Gift Wraps
Baskets & Bows

Gift Wraps
Baskets & Bows

GALWAY COUNTY LIBRARIES

 PHOENIX ILLUSTRATED

First published in 1995
by George Weidenfeld & Nicolson Ltd

This paperback edition first published in 1997 by
Phoenix Illustrated
Orion Publishing Group, Orion House
5, Upper St. Martin's Lane
London WC2H 9EA

British Library Cataloguing-in-Publication Data
A catalogue record for this book is available from
the British Library

ISBN 0-75380-223-6

Designed by Thumb Design
Edited by Alison Wormleighton
Photographs by Nadia Mackenzie
Styled by Mary Norden

Printed and bound in Italy

CONTENTS

INTRODUCTION

WHILE I WAS WORKING ON THIS BOOK, several people showed surprise when I mentioned the subject. 'A whole book about gift wrapping?' 'What is there to say?' 'Do people really bother about gift wrapping?' and the question that perplexed me the most, 'Why put all that time and effort into wrapping it so beautifully for it all then to be pulled apart?'

But is it not those presents wrapped with thought and a little imagination, however simply done, that one remembers with pleasure? Everyone loves receiving presents, and all the more if they are exquisitely wrapped. When people prepare a meal or a dinner party for a special occasion, they often will spend hours preparing and garnishing the food as well as the table, for it all then to be consumed. But people enjoy and remember the occasion and marvel at the food.

Presents are no different, except that, contrary to what most people think, you do not need to spend hours and hours or very much money to achieve wonderful gift wrapping. It is the ideas rather than the cash that count. Often, the simplest ideas which make elegant use of original materials are the most effective.

When the book was completed and I was surrounded by a whole mass of gifts wrapped in a wealth of different materials, I was asked, 'Where do all the ideas come from?' Simply from breaking a few rules. I enjoy taking materials away from their traditional uses and adapting them. Net destined for petticoats was layered with tissue paper and shimmering ribbon for a christening gift (see pages 40-1). Fabric remnants sitting at the back of a cupboard were used to wrap bottles with style (see pages 52-3), and silver cake decorations elegantly finished gifts for an anniversary (pages 34-5).

By choosing materials that are readily available and cheap, I find I am more experimental. I am not inhibited by a fear of wasting material or of a large investment. Many of the materials in this book you may already have in your home or office. Jars of shells collected from seaside holidays, odd buttons and bits of braid and ribbon left over from sewing projects, and piles of magazines you could never bring yourself to throw away will now become stylish wraps. Learn to rummage, with an open mind, through places like haberdashery (notions) departments, hardware stores, garden centres, and junk shops.

Although there are some superb patterned wrapping papers on the market, I prefer to create my own uniquely printed paper. All the techniques in the book, from the use of potato printing to bleaching crepe paper, are very easy, and no special equipment or long lists of materials are required. If you do pattern your own paper, keep the trimming simple; for my presents wrapped in bleached paper I used household string (see pages 48-9). You want people to notice your beautiful design, not the ribbon. This also applies the other way around. A stunning bow or lavish braid is enhanced by a simple one-coloured paper.

My starting point for any gift wrapping is to think of a theme – an autumnal birthday, for example, inspired the use of fallen leaves and seed pods (see pages 72-3); while classic tweed cloth for men's clothing inspired a Father's Day wrapping idea. If you are stuck for ideas, particularly when making gift baskets (see chapter 4), themes will suggest themselves if you think about the recipients and their hobbies or interests. For a keen cook wrap presents in photocopied recipes; for a football-mad child use sheets torn from a sports magazine; for a gardener make gift tags out of empty seed packets.

The range of styles included in this book, from the use of newspapers and magazines to the making of unusual gift baskets, will, I hope, offer something for everyone and illustrate that there are indeed a multitude of ways to approach gift wrapping. Either take the ideas as you see them or, even better, let them inspire you to add your own creative input. The wonderful thing about gift wrapping is that there are no rules, except perhaps just one – it should be fun.

1

Materials & Techniques

MATERIALS

THE SELECTION OF WRAPPING papers and ribbons available today is vast, and many are truly irresistible. Yet often it's the seemingly unlikely materials – anything from comics to corrugated card – which actually produce the most satisfactory results.

PAPER

There is now a huge selection of gift wrapping paper – not just at Christmas but all year round – ranging from the simplest printed stripes and checks to the most flamboyant flower patterns and golden cherubs.

None of these glossy papers are used in this book, however, because the purpose of this book is to show you how to create your own uniquely patterned paper using different techniques. The following is a list of the different papers, all readily available, which are used in this book, but there are many more that would work equally well.

Tissue This delicate paper comes in sheets of different colours ranging from the softest pink to the deepest blue. It can be layered with other paper as well as being used to pad gift baskets and wrap bunches of flowers.

Sugar paper (Construction paper) This very inexpensive paper comes in a range of muted colours and has a softer texture than traditional wrapping paper. It is very porous, which makes it ideal for printing onto.

Crepe paper This is an incredibly versatile and inexpensive paper. There are two types – the thinner paper which is very pliable, making it ideal for bottles and other awkward shapes; and the tougher, double-sided crepe paper, which has one colour on one side and a much paler colour on the other. This is ideal for bleaching patterns (see pages 48-9).

Brown paper Never ignore this humble paper. Very economical and available everywhere, it can be transformed with the right trimmings from its humble status to one of elegance. In this book you will find lots of ideas for using brown paper in a variety of unusual and striking ways.

Cellophane This is particularly suitable for wrapping around gifts where you want to display the contents – gift baskets being the obvious example. Clear cellophane is used in this book, but it does come in other colours. It is available from art and craft shops and also florists.

Plain white paper Art shops have a good supply of large sheets of different white papers – smooth or textured, matt or glossy. For gift wrapping, choose one that is strong and opaque, but not so thick that you can't achieve crisp folds during wrapping. If you want to print on it, the paper must be porous for best results, so do not choose one with a glossy surface. Thick, textured paper and thin card are suitable for making cards, tags and carrier bags for awkward-shaped gifts.

Other wrapping materials Other textured materials include corrugated card, handmade papers and sheets of woven raffia. Though not suitable for wrapping regular shapes, these all make excellent tubes for rolling around presents or for wrapping around a bunch of flowers. Other alternative wrapping materials are wallpaper, newspaper, glossy magazines, catalogues, fabric remnants and net.

RIBBON

There is an astonishing choice of ribbons now available, in a wealth of colours, textures and patterns, from the simplest of floral and nursery prints to complex woven jacquards. Ribbon can vary in width, from the narrowest 1.5mm ($^1/_{16}$in) ribbon to the widest 8cm (3in). There is a ribbon for every occasion and for every theme or style of gift wrap.

The following is a list of the types of ribbon used in this book. There are many more ribbons on the market which are not covered here.

Wire-edged During the weaving process of this ribbon, a fine wire is woven along both edges of the ribbon. This flexible wire helps the ribbon holds its shape when made into a bow or other decorative shape.

Taffeta This type of ribbon is usually matt and the same on both sides. In addition to plain colours it comes in traditional plaids, checks and stripes. Also look out for ombre taffeta, which is colour-shaded from one edge to the other, and moiré taffeta, which shimmers with a watermark. Both types of ribbon are also available with a metallic edge, making them very suitable for opulent occasions.

Satin For the largest choice of colour and width, you can't do better than shiny satin. It is available either as single-face (shiny on one side and matt on the other) or double-face (shiny on both sides). As well as plain colours satin ribbon can be found patterned. The motif most commonly associated with patterned satin is the dot, which comes in different scales.

Grosgrain Also known as petersham, these ribbons have a distinctive crosswise rib and they are stronger and thicker to handle than most of the other ribbons, like satin and taffeta. They come in wonderfully rich colours, either plain or with a very simple pattern such as sumptuous stripes.

Velvet This classic ribbon is woven with a distinctive plush pile and dyed in deep, opulent colours. It has a right and a wrong side and looks best when used in very simple ways.

Jacquard These ribbons are patterned with motifs that are actually woven into the ribbon, and they range in complexity. Some are amazingly elaborate, involving many colours, and have the appearance of a tapestry pattern. This weaving creates a right and wrong side and also adds texture. Jacquards are good for trimming boxes, where their patterns can be seen and appreciated to the full.

Sheers Sheer ribbons produce the most romantic of bows. Fine and translucent, they shimmer with light. They may be plain or printed with delicate floral patterns, or incorporate a metallic or satin thread.

Metallics When you want to add silver or gold to your gift wrapping, metallic threads are ideal. These ribbons are woven either with metallic threads exclusively, or with a combination of metallic threads and other fibres. There are also ribbons printed with gold Christmas motifs.

Lace For a feminine-looking gift wrap, choose from the vast assortment of lace ribbon and trimming. In particular, look out for the type of lace that has eyelets through which you can weave thin satin ribbon.

Paper ribbon This inexpensive ribbon comes in a snakelike coil. After careful unravelling, the finely creased paper stretches to over 15cm (6in) in width. Cut the length you require before unrolling. It is ideal for really large bows, particularly as it comes in a range of lovely colours.

ALTERNATIVE MATERIALS

String, thin rope and raffia, though they may appear the poor relations of ribbon, are equally effective for tying and trimming presents. Raffia, as well as being sold in its natural straw colour, now comes dyed in a limited but strong colour range. You will find it in most craft shops.

String is available everywhere. It comes in various thicknesses as well as textures, ranging from a smooth, fine thread that is ideal for tags, to a coarser, almost ropelike material. If you can't find any thick string or thin rope, you can always braid several strands of string together. Both raffia and string make excellent and very economical tassels (see pages 68-9).

Hardware stores and sailing stores are a good source of rope, the latter particularly for coloured rope. Rope is useful for decorating gift baskets or wrapping around and around large bunches of flowers.

Cord ranges in width from the finest cord, which is suitable for tags, to cords of almost ropelike thicknesses. Cord is particularly good for tying around little gift bags. It's like an up-market string and does have the advantage of coming in numerous colours as well as metallics.

In addition to these traditional materials, there is a whole wealth of sewing, upholstery, household and office materials that can be used. From haberdashery (notions) departments, look out for braids, fabric remnants (which can be cut or frayed into strips), hat and dress trimmings and cord. From an upholstery shop pick up lengths of webbing (twill tape) and hessian (burlap), and from a craft shop beads, buttons, sequins and stones.

TOOLS

For most gift wrapping all you need is a good pair of scissors. However, some projects do require a few additional items of equipment, though you will probably already have them at home or in the office.

For cutting card or a potato for potato printing, you will require a scalpel (mat knife) or craft knife. There are dozens of these on the market. Possibly the best one is a slim metal scalpel with a sharp renewable blade. As soon as it starts to get blunt, change the blade – most accidents happen with a blunt knife.

If you are using a scalpel or craft knife, you will also need a cutting board. These heavy duty plastic boards come in a variety of sizes and can be found in most good craft shops. Otherwise you could use an old chopping board, a piece of wood or a thick piece of cardboard.

You will, of course, need paper scissors. In addition, pinking shears are ideal for cutting up fabric remnants for wrapping, because they not only stop the fabric from fraying, but they also create a pretty edge. These are not essential, so only invest in them if you also enjoy sewing. A very small, curved pair of scissors is useful for paper cut-outs, but, again only buy this if you are planning to do a lot of découpage. The use of florist wire requires wire cutters, otherwise you will ruin your scissors.

For making boxes, a set square (carpenter's square) and a ruler are essential. A compass is useful, though you can always use a circular object as a template.

For patterning paper you will need a range of paintbrushes. When bleaching patterns a fine brush that gives you control is important (the bleach spreads wider than the painted image), while for other techniques, like potato printing and stamping, a larger brush is required so you can apply the paint as quickly as possible. For stencilling, odd bits of textured sponge are needed.

GLUES AND TAPE

Double-sided tape – a tape that is sticky on both sides – is useful for all gift wrapping. It is placed under the flaps and overlaps of the paper rather than on top like ordinary tape, so it does not show. It is also very useful for sticking or securing little bows, leaves, buttons and other trimmings onto the parcel.

PVA glue (white glue) is a versatile and reasonably fast-drying glue that dries to a clear finish. As well as sticking on cut-outs, it can also be diluted and used as a varnish for covering découpage boxes or as a sealant, for example on flower pots before spraying with colour (see page 38).

Spray adhesives are quick and very useful. They are ideal for joining two layers of paper together, particularly if one of them is very delicate like tissue paper. It won't result in a bubbled mess. However, they should be used only in a well-ventilated area, and not near a naked flame.

PAINTS

For all the printing ideas in this book artist's acrylic paints are used. These are sold in either tubes or small pots. Acrylics are mixed with water and dry very quickly. Gouache, another water-based paint, can also be used.

For brightening up wooden boxes, buckets and pots, use emulsion (latex) or spray paint. Apply spray paint in thin coats, allowing it to dry between coats. Gloss paint can also be used.

WRAPPING

RAPPING WITH STYLE
requires no special skills or
tools, just a little care, thought and
imagination. There are a great many
different kinds of paper which can be
used, each with its own character.
But for your wrapping to be a success
there are certain factors to consider.

Perhaps the most important is the size
and shape of your gift. Thick and textured
papers are obviously not suitable for
wrapping awkward-shaped gifts. It is
better to use materials that are more
pliable and that will still look good after
wrapping. Cellophane, crepe paper and
fabric remnants are all ideal. However, for
wrapping very large presents it's often
better to forget about aiming for a crease-
free wrap and instead have fun using
pages from magazines and comics.

There is an overwhelming choice of
papers that fold neatly and firmly, and
these are ideal for classic box wrapping.
You will be able to achieve the smartest
of wrappings with very little effort.
Delicate tissue paper is ideal for small
gifts, but obviously not suitable for large,
bulky ones. Brown parcel paper and
wallpaper can both be adapted for this at
very little cost, and they can look
stunning. As with using ribbons, it is
important to play with the different types
of paper so that you learn for yourself
how each folds.

Other factors to consider when choosing
your paper for wrapping are what occasion
the gift is for and whom the gift is for.

The possible variations of gift wrapping
are endless. Shown here are the basic
techniques for classic wrapping of a square,
a rectangle and a cylinder. Once you have
mastered these, you will be able to create
your own style of wrapping, devising
innumerable variations on the theme.

You don't ever need to use expensive
wrapping paper. You could only use
white and brown paper and still achieve
the most glorious wrappings – it's not the
paper that counts, but how you use it.
You could pattern it with your own
unique designs, using techniques ranging
from potato printing to stencilling. You
could cover it with paper cut-outs or even
raffle tickets. Or you could completely
transform it with clever trimmings and
other materials from around the house
and the garden.

WRAPPING A SQUARE-ENDED BOX

1 Cut a piece of paper large
enough to go around the box
with extra for an overlap. Wrap
the paper tightly around the gift
and stick down the edges one on top of
the other, or, for a smarter and neater
effect, fold over the top edge and stick
double-sided tape underneath it, leaving a
neat fold down the centre *(above right)*.

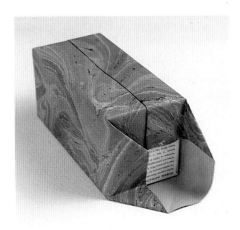

2 Cut the end flaps so that they
equal *half* the depth of the box.
With one end facing, fold the
joined section of paper down
over the end of the box to make a flap,
creasing the paper right into the corners.
Next crease the side flaps firmly, and fold
them in to meet at the centre. Bring the
resulting triangle up to meet the side flaps
at the centre. Stick the triangle down with
double-sided tape *(below)*.

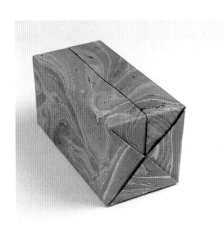

WRAPPING A CYLINDER

1 When wrapping a cylinder, avoid using very thick or textured paper as it will be difficult to fold neatly; crepe paper is ideal. Cut a piece of paper longer than the cylinder, so that there is extra paper at each end to cover half the cylinder's diameter. Make the piece of paper wide enough to go around the gift with extra for an overlap. Roll the paper tightly around the gift and stick down the edges, one on top of the other, keeping the ends free.

2 Starting with the inside flap, pleat the ends of the paper towards the centre, making small overlapping folds. It should look rather like the cross-section of an orange. Crease each fold firmly *(below)*.

3 Finish with one larger pleat and secure neatly with tape. Repeat the procedure at the other end of the cylinder, so that both ends are smooth and flat *(above right)*.

WRAPPING A BOX WITH RECTANGULAR ENDS

1 Cut a piece of paper large enough to go around the box with extra for an overlap. Wrap the paper tightly around the gift and either stick down the edges one on top of the other, or, for a smarter and neater effect, fold over the top edge of the paper and stick double-sided tape underneath it, leaving a neat fold visible at the join, down the centre of the rectangle *(below)*. (Or, to avoid having to use tape at all down the centre, fold over both edges at once.)

2 Cut the end flaps to equal the full depth of the box. With one end facing, fold the joined section of paper down over the end of the box to make a flap, creasing right into the corners.

3 Crease the side flaps firmly, and fold them in over the top flap. Bring up the bottom flap and stick it down using double-sided tape. Repeat for the other end *(below)*.

WRAPPING A SMALL, SHALLOW BOX

This style of wrapping gives a box a softer look than a classic wrap and is ideal for more delicate wrapping papers like tissue and thin crepe paper.

1 Cut a piece of paper at least $2^{1}/_{2}$ times longer than the length of the box, and wide enough to go around it with extra for an overlap. Place the gift at one end of the paper. Wrap the paper around the gift and stick down the edges along the full length of the paper *(opposite, above)*.

2 Bring up the top, keeping its edges within the edges of the gift. Softly gather up both ends of the paper, gathering the top flap slightly more for fullness. Secure with string or florist wire *(below)*.

3 Tie the gift with a bow and puff out the gathered paper. If the paper is too long, trim it down to size *(above right)*.

WRAPPING A SHALLOW SQUARE

This style of wrapping works well for all types of paper.

1 Neatly wrap a gift in patterned paper. For a shallow square, wrap as though for a box with square ends (see page 13). Cut a square piece of contrasting paper $1^1/_2$ times larger than the square gift. Place the gift in the centre of the contrasting paper with each corner touching the edge of the paper *(below)*. If the second paper is too large, trim it down.

2 Fold the paper over the gift to form four triangles. Cut a piece of ribbon slightly longer than the distance between two points. With double-sided tape, secure the ribbon at both ends under the two points *(below)*, thus pulling the flaps towards each other.

3 Cut two pieces of ribbon long enough to tie into a bow. With double-sided tape, stick one end of each under the remaining points. Pull the flaps together and tie the ribbons into a bow *(below)*.

TYING BOWS

A BOW SHOULD ENHANCE not only the ribbon it is made of, but also the style of the wrapped gift it is decorating. However simple, it can transform a quite ordinary gift into something very special.

The size of the bow in relation to that of the present is also very important. A small regular-shaped gift which is crisply wrapped in checks or plaids needs no more than a very simple classic bow, while a larger present wrapped in tissue, lace and net obviously requires something larger and more showy to enhance the lavish wrapping.

Another important factor in the making of bows is the choice of colour. You should consider not only the colours and textures of the wrapping materials, but also the occasion for which the gift is intended. For example, metallic ribbons in old gold, taffeta patterned with red and green plaids, and deep, richly coloured velvets are all ideally suited to the opulence of Christmas.

Like choosing flowers, your choice of colour will often be dictated by the time of year. In spring you could use fresh colours, like yellow and blue. In the summer, try hotter colours and then in autumn go for softer, more muted colours. Christmas will bring a blaze of jewel-like colour.

The number of different bow styles can be rather daunting. Here, four different types of fancy bows are demonstrated – the double bow, the picture bow, the flat multi-bow and the full double multi-bow. All use the simplest techniques. Once you have learned how to make these, you will be able to create your own bows. Use these bows as a starting point.

There is a vast, almost overwhelming choice of ribbon now available. Don't be intimidated by it all – play with the different types to learn how they fold and tie, and what style of bow they are best suited to. For example, wired ribbon holds its shape, making it suitable for the most lavish of bows. A ribbon like grosgrain, on the other hand, which is heavier because of its distinctive crosswise rib, is much less versatile and so is best kept for simpler bows. Velvet, with its plush pile, makes richer, more formal bows while a shimmering, translucent ribbon like gauze makes wonderfully romantic bows. As a general rule, heavier ribbons are best suited to more tailored flat bows, while lighter-weight ribbons, which can be easily looped and twisted, are much more versatile and can be used to create fuller bows.

Experiment with different colours and widths of ribbon. Use them in layers for opulence, and colour-coordinate them for sophistication. Also put different textured ribbons together. The double multi-bow

shown on page 21 was made from combining a shimmering gauze with a wired taffeta. The more you experiment, the more you will be inspired.

The tails of a ribbon are as important as the loops. Cut too short, they will create an unbalanced bow. If you are unsure what length they should be, plan them longer. You can always cut them shorter after the bow has been tied. The tail ends should be cut either diagonally or in an inverted 'V'. This is not just for decorative reasons but because it prevents a woven ribbon from fraying.

If you plan to make a lot of bows, it is worth buying a bowmaker. This simple but ingenious tool consists of a wooden base with two pegs that can be moved to different positions, depending on what size of bow is required. You can use it with the narrowest ribbon to create hundreds of tiny bows, each one a consistent shape and size, or it can be adjusted to take the widest ribbon.

Bows can be attached to a gift either with double-sided tape or with a piece of florist wire, narrow ribbon or cord which has been threaded through the back of the bow and then twisted or tied around part of the gift.

Despite the multitude of possibilities, don't forget the good old classic bow, the first bow children learn to tie. Of all the bows, this is the most versatile, and the one you'll return to again and again.

In addition to ribbon, there are alternative materials that can be used. Fabric is an obvious and inexpensive choice. Cut strips from fabric remnants or even old sheets and prettily patterned discarded clothes. Use pinking shears, not only to prevent fraying but also to give a decorative edge. The size of the bow will depend on the width and length of the strips. Experiment with string to find the right length.

To stiffen a bow made from fabric, mix flour and water to the consistency of thin cream, beating well to eliminate lumps, and dip the bow into the paste. Squeeze gently to remove excess liquid. Place the dipped bow onto a baking tray, arranging it in a pleasing shape. Place in a very cool oven for 10–15 minutes, turning the bow over and adjusting it if necessary. Spray with colour.

Other materials, such as raffia, string and paper ribbon, are more effective when used for very simple bows or even just knotted. Bows can also be made from a combination of conventional ribbon and alternative materials – see, for example, the simple raffia bow layered onto a gauze multi-bow (page 36).

The design possibilities of bow-making and the use of ribbon can be greatly increased with sewing, but for the purposes of this book, the bows have been made without the use of needle and thread. Ribbons can be ruffled and

gathered simply by stitching a line of gathering stitches (either by hand or by machine) down the centre or along one edge of the ribbon. Pleated and intricately folded bows can maintain their shape with just a few stitches at the back of the bow. If you are interested in exploring bow-making techniques even more, there are numerous books on the market about ribboncraft, which is enjoying a revival.

DOUBLE BOW

The instructions are for using three contrasting ribbons, but you could use the same ribbon for each loop, if you prefer.

1 Cut a 30cm (12in) length of 5cm (2in) wide wired ribbon. Fold it to form a loop, with the two ends slightly overlapping at the centre back of the loop. Repeat with a 25cm (10in) length of 2.5cm (1in) wide wired ribbon in a contrasting colour. Place this second loop on top of the first. Cut a 25cm (10in) piece of 2.5cm (1in) wide ribbon in a third colour or pattern. Fold this over both the loops as shown *(below)*.

2 Tie the third ribbon around the two loops into a knot *(below)*. Pull tight and move the knot to the back, making sure that the loop ends are caught.

3 Cut each of the tail ends of the bow in an inverted 'V'. Puff out the loops so that they don't look flat *(below)*.

4 To secure the bow onto a gift, either thread a small piece of florist wire behind the knot or use double-sided tape.

PICTURE BOW

1 Cut two 30cm (12in) lengths of 5cm (2in) wide wired ribbon. Fold each one into loops, with the two ends slightly overlapping at the centre back of the loop. Place the two loops one on top of the other. Cut a 35cm (14in) length of 5cm (2in) wide ribbon. Fold it in half and place it behind the two loops as shown *(below)*.

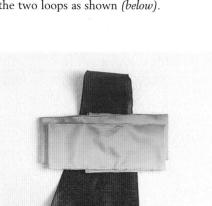

2 Cut two pieces of gold cord or very thin ribbon. Wrap one piece diagonally across the centre of the bow and knot tightly at the back. At this stage the bow will look very crooked. Repeat with the second piece of gold cord, crossing it in the opposite direction to the first piece *(above right)*.

3 Make sure the loop ends are firmly caught behind the cord. Do not trim the cord ends at this stage – they are useful for securing the bow to the gift. Cut the tail ends in an inverted 'V'. Puff out the loops *(below)*.

FLAT MULTI-BOW

This bow is best made with ribbon no thinner than 1.5cm (⁵⁄₈in). If you prefer a very full bow, add more loops.

1 Cut a 90cm (36in) length of 2.5cm (1in) wide wired ribbon. Working on a flat surface, place the ribbon horizontally in front of you. Fold the ribbon 15cm (6in) from the right-hand edge to form the first loop. Fold the ribbon after another 15cm (6in), thus returning the ribbon to the left and forming a second loop. Repeat this process, making the next two loops 12.5cm (5in) apart and the last two loops 10cm (4in) apart. You now have three sets of loops of varying length *(below)*. Do not cut the remaining ribbon.

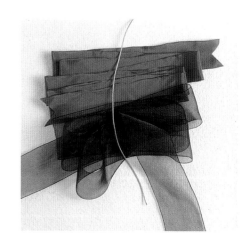

2 To finish the bow, cut a piece of cord or florist wire, tie it around the centre of the ribbon and knot or twist it to secure *(below)*.

3 Trim the bow tails to equal length and cut the ends in an inverted 'V'. Puff up and fan out the loops *(below)*.

DOUBLE MULTI-BOW

This bow is best made with ribbon wider than 2.5cm (1in).

1 Cut two 2.2m (90in) lengths of two different ribbons, each 5cm (2in) wide. Here, a wired ribbon and a shimmering gauze ribbon have been used. Working on a flat surface, place one of the ribbons horizontally in front of you. Fold the ribbon 25cm (10in) from the right-hand edge to form the first loop. Fold the ribbon after another 25cm (10in), thus returning the ribbon to the left and forming a second loop. Repeat this process until you have four sets of loops, each of equal length. Repeat with the second ribbon. Now cut a piece of cord or florist wire *(below)*.

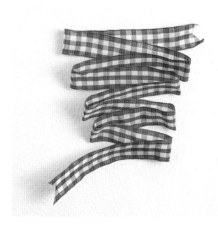

2 Place the colour you want in the centre of the bow on top of the other ribbon. Take the piece of cord or florist wire, tie it around the centre of the ribbon and knot or twist it to secure *(below)*.

3 Cut all the bow ends in an inverted 'V'. Arrange the loops in a rosette, puffing them up so the bow is very full *(below)*.

Special Occasions

ON A FESTIVE NOTE

UPDATE TRADITIONAL Christmas wrappings and create a festive ambience with a flourish of musical notes. Sheet music enlarged on a photocopier provides a crisp accompaniment to seasonal red and gold trimmings.

MATERIALS

Sheet music
Thick red crepe paper
Florist wire
Gold wired ribbon
Double-sided tape
Cellophane tape
Red ribbon
Gold angel decorations (optional)

1 Using a photocopier, enlarge the sheet music again and again until the music is as large as you require. For bulky presents that need really large sheets of wrapping paper, you may need to tape several pieces of photocopied music together. Neatly wrap the gifts using the photocopied sheets.

2 To make a fan, cut out a piece of red crepe paper 15cm (6in) wide by 23cm (9in) high (or a different size if you prefer). Fold the paper widthwise, working the creases backward and forward so that every other crease faces up, and the alternate ones face down. This will give an accordion-pleated effect. When folding, it is helpful to crease each fold well with your thumbnail. (If you are unsure of the technique, practise first with a sheet of plain paper.) Start and finish with the pleats facing down. If after pleating the length of paper, you find that you are going to finish with a pleat facing up, just cut off the last pleat. Hold the pleated paper closed while you wrap and tie a piece of florist wire around the centre. Gently fan out the paper until you have almost a full circle of pleats. Decorate the fan with gold wired ribbon and stick it to the present with double-sided tape.

3 To make a scroll, cut a piece of photocopied music 10cm (4in) square. Roll it up and secure with cellophane tape, then decorate with red ribbon. Attach the scroll to the bow with florist wire. If you wish, you could, tie gold angel decorations to the bow too.

VARIATIONS

• For a more elaborate-looking fan, use photocopied music instead of red crepe paper. Before you pleat the paper, glue strips of gold paper or 1.5cm (5/8in) wide gold cake-decorating ribbon down both sides of the music. Finish with a gold wired ribbon. These fans look stunning decorating gifts wrapped in plain red paper.

• Alternatively, point the pleats. This is done after tying with wire, but before the pleated paper is opened up. Cut the ends into points, cutting through all layers at once. For a lace effect, cut-outs can be made into the edges of the folds when the fan is still closed.

• Sometimes you can find old sheet music for next to nothing in junk shops. Use this instead of photocopied music for wrapping small gifts, covering little boxes (see pages 88-9) or making old-fashioned sweet (candy) boxes and cones (see pages 92-3).

• Instead of tying the pleated paper in the middle, staple it at one end.

• In addition to making scrolls and fans as decorative finishes, try wrapping small, empty matchboxes or even stock (bouillon) cubes in sheet music. Tie the 'parcels' with gold thread and then attach them to the gift.

STAR-STUDDED GIFTS

LEARN TO USE the amazingly simple technique of stamping and your gifts are sure to play a starring role. Continue the theme with cut-out stars used in a variety of dramatic ways.

Using a stamp is remarkably easy and very effective. No special skills are required, and a sheet of plain wrapping paper can be covered in seconds. Stamps can be used with most kinds of craft paints and paper, but a porous surface gives the best results, so avoid paper with a glossy sheen. Although paint can be applied to the stencil with a brush, for large quantities of paper a paint roller or a stamp pad is easier. These are widely available from craft shops or by mail order, along with a huge selection of different-shaped stamps.

MATERIALS

White matt paper
Paintbrush, roller or paint pad
Gold paint
Star stamp

STAMPING STARS

1 Before stamping, practise on a spare piece of paper similar to the paper you want to decorate. Whether using a brush, a roller or a paint pad to apply the colour, always coat the stamp evenly with paint. Don't apply too much, or it will smudge.

2 After applying the paint, press the stamp down firmly onto the paper then lift it off with a steady hand. The stamp must be recoated with paint before each impression. For best results, use the stamps on a flat, smooth surface.

3 Apply the motif randomly across the paper or in rows. If you are unsure about using the stamp freehand, mark out the position of the stars with a soft pencil first.

4 Stamp stars in rows along long strips of paper or fabric, and use these strips instead of ribbon to decorate the wrapped parcel.

VARIATIONS

• Ring the changes with colour – gold stars on deep ultramarine blue look stunning – as well as different types of textured paper. Delicate sheets of tissue paper covered in stars are almost too good to use.

• Look out for other stamps and cover your presents with cherubs, moons and fleurs-de-lys. Or for a cruder but equally effective look, make your own stamps out of potatoes (see pages 74-5).

• To wrap an awkward shape, make a fabric bag (see pages 60-1) and stamp it with stars using fabric paint. Tie it closed with ribbon decorated with more stars.

STAR CUT-OUTS

1 Cut stars out of white paper and stick them at random onto gold wrapping paper. You might find it easier to apply the stars after you have wrapped the gift. Vary the size of the stars as well as the style by using the templates at the end of the book.

2 Make star-shaped tags from thin gold card. If you cannot find any, glue gold paper to thin white cardboard, then cut out the stars. Tie them onto the parcel with gold cord.

3 For dramatic tags or just pure decoration, pleat a piece of paper into a fan (see pages 24-5) and decorate this with star stickers. The same star stickers can also be used to decorate white parcel tags. At Easter they can adorn any plain Easter egg (even hard-boiled eggs) – or be stuck at random over clear or coloured cellophane used to wrap a bunch of flowers. Wrap the stems with cord, and finish with one large star, cut out of card.

4 For something less busy, wrap a present in plain gold paper, tie it with wide ribbon or stripes of crepe paper and finish with one large star cut out of thin card and stuck in the middle. Simple but chic.

CHRISTMAS JEWELS

BREAK FROM THE TRADITIONAL Christmas colours of scarlet and green and make your own gift wraps glitter with a vibrant mix of crepe paper bejewelled with sequins, braids, beads and gold cord. For those who love to rummage, this project is a joy. Raid haberdashery (notions) departments and if you can't find crepe paper, substitute something else so long as it's bright. Offcuts of velvet, silk and satin make truly opulent gift wraps.

Rather than layering expensive ribbon over wider ribbon, an equally effective idea is to cut out strips of contrasting paper or fabric wider than your finishing braid and wrap these around your present before you add the final trimming.

Dramatic contrasts of colour in your gift wrapping can also be created by paper cut-outs. Using a contrasting-coloured paper to the one you have wrapped your gift in, fold the paper in half repeatedly. The more the paper is folded, the more elaborate the cut-outs will be, but make sure that the paper is not too thick to cut. Using a small, sharp pair of scissors, cut out small sections of the paper along the folded line. Gently unfold the cut paper and carefully wrap it around the gift.

Yet another way to add to the opulence of your gifts is to use glitter. Simply lay out a sheet of plain paper and with a paintbrush dab on small circles of glue at random. (If you prefer, use a bottle of glue with a fine nozzle.) Now sprinkle glitter across from side to side, making sure that all the glue is covered. Tip the excess glitter back into its container. Leave to dry before using. This process can also be done after a gift has been wrapped. Stand the wrapped present on newspaper and work on one side at a time, pressing the glitter into the glue with your finger. To embellish your paper still further, stick a bead, a large sequin, a rhinestone, or other glass 'jewel' into the centre of each glittering circle.

GOLDEN CHRISTMAS

IMAGINE CHRISTMAS without touches of shimmering gold – it is almost as unthinkable as Christmas without a festive tree. Ever since the Magi brought gold, frankincense and myrrh to the baby Jesus, gold has been the colour of Christmas. Richly luxurious, its glittering theatricality can instantly transform a gift, adding dramatic impact to otherwise unremarkable materials.

Creating a gold theme for your Christmas wraps, or in fact for any time of the year, is relatively easy. In addition to a vast assortment of gold papers and ribbons, a wide range of gold paints and markers is now easily available. You can easily transform ordinary household objects as well as materials from the garden into glittering Christmas decorations with no more than a can of gold spray. The instructions and suggestions given here relate to the gift wraps which are shown opposite and on pages 2 and 22-30.

For an elegant way of wrapping chocolates or small, awkwardly shaped gifts, surround them in layers of cellophane and gold lace or net (see pages 22-3). Cut a circle of cellophane at least two to three times bigger than your gift. Place the gift in the centre of the cellophane and bunch it up in the middle. Secure with an elastic band (rubber band). Repeat with a piece of gold net or lace. Cover the bands with a gold cord or ribbon tied into a bow, and add a couple of tassels. Alternatively, omit the net or lace and leave the cellophane showing. Or wrap your gifts in brown paper instead of cellophane, and cover this with net or lace, for an unusual and striking contrast.

If you have a gift that can be divided into three different boxes, or regular shapes, preferably of different sizes, wrap each box in a different gold paper. Or for added texture, wrap them first in brown paper and then add a layer of either gold lace or net. Stack the three boxes and tie together with extra-wide wired gold ribbon, finishing with a bow on top. Be dramatic and add a

multi-bow (see pages 20-21) made out of contrasting ribbon and, if desired, add one or two Christmas tree decorations, fastened to the bow with florist wire.

Instead of Christmas tree decorations, you could adorn your gifts with seed pods, fir cones, leaves and even wheat spikelets, all sprayed gold. Before applying the paint, make sure that the objects to be sprayed are completely dry. Apply the gold spray in thin coats, allowing it to dry between coats and gradually building up to the depth of colour you require. For smart tags and greetings cards, cut out pieces of white card and glue a gold-sprayed leaf to the centre.

If you need a really large gold bow, the easiest and cheapest way to do this is to make it out of a length of gold fabric or even white crepe paper and then spray it with gold paint. Stiffening fabric bows by dipping them in a mixture of flour and water and then briefly drying them in the oven (see page 19) before spraying them gold is extremely effective. This technique can be used for stiffening fabric bows of all sizes and is ideal for Christmas tree bows in particular.

Golden tassels are one of the most luxurious finishes you can give a present. They look particularly good when used to dress a wrapped bottle. You can either buy them ready-made or be economical and make them (see pages 68-9) out of gold knitting thread, which is just as effective as many of the other more expensive yarns.

Make your own golden wrapping paper. One of the quickest and easiest techniques is sponging. Pour gold craft paint into a saucer. Dip a small piece of natural sponge into the paint and then lightly dab it at random all over a piece of plain paper - brown parcel paper or chocolate-coloured tissue paper is ideal as a base. Another quick technique is spattering. This is best done outside. Simply dip a paintbrush in gold paint and then with a flicking action shake it across your paper, for a lovely sparkly effect.

WEDDING ROSES

COVER YOUR GIFTS with a magnificent display of roses that will give instant pleasure but will last for ever.

Ribbon doesn't have to be restricted to making bows - it can also be used to make clever imitations of flowers. Ribbon flowers can be very elaborate or classically simple. These ribbon roses are made from just one continuous strip of ribbon and there is no sewing involved, so they are incredibly quick to make.

One flower is usually enough to decorate a small gift. But for larger gifts and special occasions, two or three roses together look good, particularly if you use different-coloured ribbons that blend beautifully together.

The elegant wedding wraps shown here consist of bags made from shimmering crushed velvet and satin (see pages 60-1). To match the sophisticated tones of the fabric bags, ribbons in shades of grey and brown with cream were used for the roses.

For more realistic-looking flowers, you could imitate the colours of old roses with a blend of soft, faded pinks and cream, or perhaps rich, sumptuous reds combined with magenta and purple.

For an opulent finishing touch, try adding a rose to the centre of a bow in a contrasting colour.

MATERIALS

For each rose
30cm (12in) of 5cm (2in) wide wired ribbon

1 Make a knot as close as possible to one end of the ribbon. At the opposite end, pull out the wire along one edge, so that the ribbon starts to ruffle.

2 As you continue to pull the wire out with one hand, gently tease back the ruffles towards the knot with the other hand. Pull until the length of ribbon is completely gathered.

3 Working as closely as possible to the knot, wind the gathered edge around and around. Wind the remaining wire around several times to secure.

4 Do not cut off the excess wire. Gently tease out the flower so it looks more like a bloom than a bud, and then use the excess wire as a means of attaching the flower to the gift.

VARIATIONS

• Experiment with different widths and lengths of ribbon: the size of a ribbon flower depends on both these factors. Instead of grouping two or three ribbon roses together, for example, you could make just one large rose using 60cm (24in) of 10cm (4in) wide ribbon. As a general guide, the length should be six times the width. For a very full rose cut the ribbon even longer.

• For a more spectacular rose, use two different-coloured ribbons within one flower. Make one rose with one colour and then gather the second ribbon and wrap it around the first. Secure the two together by winding the excess of the second ribbon around both knots. Tease out the ribbon. This technique looks glorious (and very realistic) when worked with two different shades of pink or of yellow. Use the darker shade for the centre of the flower.

• Experiment with unwired ribbon and strips of fabric (cutting one edge with pinking shears for a decorative finish). Run a row of small stitches along one edge, using either a sewing machine or working by hand. Knot securely at one end and complete as above. Use the excess thread to work a few stitches to hold the flower in shape.

ANNIVERSARY COLOURS

THE STYLISH ALTERNATIVE to ribbons and bows is to trim special gifts with a clever mix of cake decorations. A wide variety of decorations come in both silver and gold, which makes them perfect for wrapping gifts for the 25th and 50th wedding anniversaries.

Look out for wired floral leaves (available in an assortment of metallic colours), paper ribbons to match, paper cake frills with printed greetings, doilies in a multitude of delicate lace patterns as well as sizes, and of course a mass of cake-top ornaments and letterings.

Rather than using all silver or gold, you could add another colour. For example, blue looks very regal with silver, as does a faded green.

MATERIALS

Silver or gold wrapping paper
Silver or gold doilies
Double-sided tape (optional)
Silver or gold ribbon or paper cake edging
Wired rose, fern and ivy leaves, all in silver or gold

1 If the gift is not a regular shape, place it in a box (see pages 58-9) and neatly wrap it in silver or gold paper. You may wish to add a circular doily of the same colour. It doesn't matter if the doily only wraps around part of the gift, or even just sits on top of the parcel – it will create the desired effect. If necessary, secure the doily with a couple of pieces of double-sided tape.

2 Either tie ribbon around the gift, fastening it in a bow, or cut two pieces of cake edging to fit around the box, forming a cross on top. Secure centrally on the top with tape.

3 Decorate the parcel with wired leaves, twisting the wire stems together and tucking them under the ribbon or edging. Cut off the excess wire if there is too much. Alternatively, place just one leaf in the centre of a bow, cut off the wire stem and secure with double-sided tape.

VARIATIONS

Instead of using plain metallic paper, you could create your own patterned paper. In addition to stencilling, stamping, spattering or sponging, and bleaching (see pages 54-5, 26-7, 31 and 48-9 respectively), the following techniques will work well.

• Doilies can be used very effectively as stencils to create patterned paper. Because this technique involves spray painting, it is advisable to work in a well-ventilated room – or outside – and to protect the surrounding surfaces with newspaper. Lay pieces of plain white paper on a flat surface (avoiding paper with a glossy sheen). Onto each one, place a large doily. It is helpful, though not essential, to spray a very fine layer of adhesive onto the back of the doily, to hold it in position as you apply the colour. Otherwise, hold the doily with one hand while you work. Using silver or gold spray, gently spray backwards and forwards across each doily until the paper is covered. Allow the paint to dry before you remove the doilies. This will prevent you from smudging the pattern.

• Another method, sponging, is quick and easy and very effective. Pour silver or gold paint into a saucer or old container. Dip a small piece of natural sponge into the paint, and then lightly dab at random all over a piece of plain paper. White tissue paper looks beautiful covered in this way, especially if you place it over a contrasting colour, such as purple.

A ROSE FOR MOTHER'S DAY

GATHER LAYERS OF TISSUE paper and net around a Mother's Day gift and adorn it with a faded rose and a shimmering bow.

This gift wrap works well and looks interesting because it combines different-textured materials – silk contrasting with raffia, and net with tissue. This consideration is useful to remember when collecting materials not just for this particular wrap but for all sorts of occasions.

MATERIALS

Tissue paper
Net
Raffia
Gauze ribbon
Fabric or paper rose

1 Cut two sheets of tissue paper and a piece of net at least 2–2^1/$_2$ times bigger than the object. It is always better to cut it too large at this stage, as you can trim it down later. Here a beautiful soft brown tissue paper has been used with cream net.

2 Place the gift in the middle of the tissue paper, gather or pleat it up over the present and lightly secure with string.

Repeat with the net. Remove the string from around the tissue paper and use it to tie all the layers together.

3 Tie the gauze ribbon around the neck of the present and make a large floppy bow. On top of this tie a simple raffia bow, using several strands of raffia together. After tying, trim any loose strands. Arrange the two bows so that they sit nicely together.

4 If the rose has a long stem, trim it to 5cm (2in). To secure the rose to the front of the gift, gently push the rose stem behind the knot of the ribbon.

VARIATIONS

• Both tissue paper and net come in a vast array of colours - from the palest of pinks to the deepest of blues, so experiment with different colours. For this Mother's Day wrap, the faded pinks and browns give a soft, almost antique feel, reminiscent of a bowl of dried rose petals. For a traditional Christmas wrap, try red tissue paper with green net, or vice-versa, or a tartan bow with a twist of ivy. For an Easter gift, bright yellow tissue with cream net, finished with a blue bow and yellow raffia, looks fresh. For an autumn birthday, choose shades of reds, oranges and yellows.

• You could even try layering different shades of tissue paper, rather than limiting yourself to just one shade. For a truly extravagant look, use three or even four layers.

• Explore the bridal fabric section of your local store and collect not just plain net but also patterned – spotted net is the most popular – as well as other stiff, inexpensive fabrics.

• Instead of fabric flowers, you could use dried flowers – one large blue hydrangea looks magnificent – or make a tiny posy of red roses with lavender, tied with raffia. Alternatively, add a freshly picked flower from the garden, or an exotic bloom from your local florist.

• Replace the outer layer of net with clear cellophane. Before tying it at the neck of the present, scatter a few dried flower heads or petals between the cellophane and the tissue paper so they are visible. Or simply scatter fresh petals around the gift or on the tea tray.

EASTER LAURELS

TRANSFORM ORDINARY FLOWERPOTS into glittering bearers of Easter eggs with just a lick of gold paint and a few laurel leaves. Yellow is the colour usually associated with Easter, but why not break with tradition and opt for a more regal effect with gold and dark green?

In the month before Easter look out for large chocolate eggs plainly wrapped in gold foil. (Chocolate shops usually sell them, or if not, they will happily place an order.) To decorate your eggs, choose glossy leaves which are pliable and strong. Laurel leaves are ideal.

Some of the Easter eggs can be placed in gold flowerpots. The quickest and easiest way to cover a pot in gold is to use gold spray. First prime the pot with PVA adhesive (white glue), to make the surface non-porous and give a deeper, richer gold. Allow this to dry then spray the pot evenly and in thin coats, allowing it to dry between coats. Two layers are usually enough unless you want a rich covering.

Paint a line of glue around the inside of the rim and leave it to dry until it is just tacky. Now position the laurel leaves around the inner rim, placing the wrong side of the leaves in the glue. Bend the leaves over to the right side of the pot and secure with a simple raffia bow.

Alternatively, use long, narrow leaves and cover the whole pot. Fill your pots with not just one large egg, but also several smaller eggs, or even lots of tiny solid chocolate eggs.

Quicker and cheaper than gilding flowerpots is to make a cardboard tube large enough to hold the egg upright. Make sure the tube is at least 4cm (1 1/2 in) shorter than your leaves. To decorate it, apply glue or double-sided tape all around the centre of the tube and stick on the leaves, overlapping them so that the cardboard is not visible. At this stage the leaves will extend beyond both ends of the tube. Trim off the excess leaves at the bottom edge so that the tube will stand.

CHRISTENING LACE

FOR A REALLY SPECIAL DAY, what could be nicer than a present wrapped in a froth of net over delicate layers of tissue paper and finished with a shimmering bow?

MATERIALS

Coloured tissue paper
White tissue paper or very thin textured
white paper
Net
4cm (1¹/₂ in) wide lace
Wired ribbon
Thin white ribbon
Double-sided tape

1 Place the gift in a simple cardboard box (to make a box, see pg 58), then neatly wrap it in coloured tissue paper. Here, three sheets of pale lilac tissue paper have been used, but you might wish to be more traditional and have pale blue for a boy or pink for a girl. Finish with a sheet of textured, but thin and almost transparent paper in white.

2 Cut two pieces of lace to fit around the box diagonally *(above right)*. Secure the ends neatly at the back with double-sided tape. If the lace is inclined to slip, secure it at each corner of the box with small pieces of double-sided tape discreetly placed underneath the lace.

3 Cut a piece of net at least twice the width of the box and long enough to wrap around the box plus a 5cm (2 in) allowance at each end. Place the gift in the centre of the net. Gather up each end of its length to meet in the middle of the box and secure with a thin ribbon. If you find it easier, secure the net first with an elastic band (rubber band). Trim away any excess net. Arrange the gathered net evenly across the width *(below)*.

4 Finish the present with a large multi-bow (see page 21), made from wide wired ribbon, fanning out the loops gracefully over the top of the present.

VARIATIONS

• For a long narrow present, you could wrap and gather three pieces of net around the box and have three glorious bows arranged down its length, instead of one bow in the centre. But keep the bows small or it could look too much.

• For a more spectacular finish to your gift, cut the net adding an extra 25–35cm (10–14 in) to the length. Do not trim the net after securing it at the centre. Add the finishing bow and then arrange both so that the net and ribbons are well balanced.

• Both net and tissue paper come in a multitude of colours so do experiment with different colour shades, as well as different papers and fabrics. Blue tissue paper, pink net and a navy bow look stunning, as does brown paper under gold net topped with a maroon ribbon.

• Look out for patterned net, in particular the classic spotted net used for wedding veils and hats.

• Instead of net, use other stiff, inexpensive fabrics and remnants of lace fabric. Discarded lace curtains are ideal, particularly for larger presents.

VALENTINE HEARTS & FLOWERS

CREATE ROMANTIC GIFT wraps by combining the two traditional elements of Valentine's day – hearts and roses.

Rather than covering your gifts just with plain red hearts, you can actually bring together the hearts and roses themes by decorating your gifts with floral hearts. Simply cut heart shapes out of old rose catalogues, selecting pictures of red or deep pink roses.

MATERIALS

Plain white paper
Old rose catalogue
PVA adhesive (white glue)
Thin red ribbon
Red crepe paper
Strong red paper
Thin white ribbon
White corrugated card
Wide white ribbon
White card

1 For a long, narrow Valentine present, first wrap the gift in white paper. Using the template on page 108, neatly cut out hearts from rose pictures. Apply a thin layer of glue to the wrong side of the hearts and stick them on down the centre of the parcel, spacing them evenly. In between each heart, tie a small bow using thin red ribbon. Keep the bows small or it could look too much.

2 For a Valentine gift bag, make a bag out of strong red paper (see pages 90-1) but do not punch holes at the top. Instead, pinch the top edges together and fold over twice, towards the front of the bag. Tie a thin white ribbon around the bag, tying it in a small bow or knot at the front of the bag near the top. This will hold the turn-over in place. Cut a square of corrugated white card to fit on the front of the bag. Cut out a heart from a red rose picture. Using a thin layer of glue, stick the heart onto the corrugated card. Now stick the card onto the front of the bag over the ribbon.

3 For a low cylindrical gift, first wrap the gift in red crepe paper (see page 13). Tie a wide white ribbon around the present, in both directions, finishing with a bow on top. From white paper, cut out four diamonds which measure as near to the height as possible without overlapping each other. Neatly cut out four hearts from rose pictures, small enough to fit into the diamonds. Using thin layers of glue, stick the heart onto the paper diamond, and each diamond onto one side of the present, over the ribbon.

4 For a tall cylindrical present, cut out hearts from rose pictures, stick them onto plain white paper and then cut around the shape, leaving a border of white all around each heart. Stick the hearts onto the side of the gift, before tying with wide white ribbon.

5 Make heart-shaped tags as in step 4, but instead of sticking the floral hearts onto paper, stick them onto white card. Once cut out, punch a hole near the top and attach with thin red ribbon.

VARIATIONS

• Decorate plain white paper with red hearts printed with either a potato print (see pages 74-5) or by stencilling (see pages 54-5). Ring the changes and print white hearts onto red paper, or break with tradition and choose completely different colours for your valentine. Print gold hearts onto brown or black paper, or for a fresh, Scandinavian feel, blue hearts on white, or white on blue.

SUITED TO FATHER'S DAY

CRISP CHECKS, BOLD COLOURS and neat bows make a perfect combination for an ultra-smart Father's Day. The inspiration for this idea came from a 1940s black-and-white gangster movie. All the men were wearing immaculate suits, each one made in a different classic cloth – herringbone, houndstooth, pinstripe, Prince of Wales check.

Gangsters may seem an unlikely starting point for Father's Day, but traditional men's fabrics are well suited for macho-looking gift wraps. Tailors and dressmakers usually have bags and bags of fabric remnants, which they are only too happy to give away, or sell very cheaply. Choose remnants in black-and-white, then, as a contrast, combine them with paper in bright, vivid colours.

Decorate the wrapped gifts with either gingham or plain black ribbon or cord tied into simple, neat bows. Black raffia tassels (see pages 68-9) can be used instead of bows. For an awkward-shaped gift, either gather it up in fabric or place in a box covered in one of the classic black-and-white tweeds and trimmed with black braid (see page 102). For a large box you could use a different black-and-white pattern on each side. This patchwork effect might look messy on a small box. Men's fabrics are also ideal for wrapping up bottles (see pages 52-3). Don't forget, in addition to black-and-white woven fabrics, there are hundreds of other tweeds to choose from.

In complete contrast, another idea for Father's Day is to incorporate an old tie into the wrapping. This is particularly fun if you are actually giving a new tie as a gift. Wrap the gift in tissue paper and place it in a small box. The box can be either plain white or covered in a coloured paper (see pages 102-3) that complements the colouring of the old tie. Wrap the tie around the box and tie it into a big floppy bow.

3

Themes

CREPE PAPER PATTERNS

NOTHING COULD BE EASIER or more fun than creating dramatic wraps by bleaching out your own patterns from crepe paper.

Simple geometric motifs – circles, stars, zig-zags, squares – used randomly across the paper or in rows give the most effective patterns. You could also try writing large random words to give the effect of paper covered in calligraphy.

MATERIALS

Crepe paper
Household bleach
Small paintbrush
Old jar top
String
Dried leaves (optional)

1 Lay the crepe paper flat on several sheets of newspaper or a plastic sheet. Sometimes it helps to gently flatten out the fullness and secure the corners with tape.

2 Into the jar lid pour a small quantity of bleach and add a few drops of water (the more water you add the weaker the design). Dip in the paintbrush and then gently shake to remove excess. To prevent too much bleeding of bleach, it is best to work quickly and lightly.

3 Paint on the shape freehand. For an evenly bleached pattern, dip the paintbrush into the bleach after each shape. Or, for a more uneven, almost faded pattern (see circles on red, opposite) work until the paintbrush is almost dry, before re-dipping the brush into the bleach. Some colours react faster and more strongly to bleach than others, where the effect is softer and more gradual.

An alternative way of patterning paper with bleach is to place objects on the paper and paint around the shapes. For example, place leaves at random on a piece of crepe paper and quickly paint around each one, holding it in position with your finger. Simple, flat-shaped leaves are best, such as ivy and laurel. For a more abstract pattern you could overlap some of the leaves, and by varying the strength of the bleach create a wonderful pattern of falling leaves. In addition to leaves you could use paint around biscuit cutters. Paper covered in gingerbread men would be fun for a child's gift.

Another equally effective technique is to spatter patterns. Dip the paintbrush into the bleach and then with a flicking movement shake it across the paper. Repeat several times from different angles. (This is best done outside or in an area which is well covered with newspaper.)

You can also bleach out patterns using the stencilling technique. Cake doilies and bleach will create glorious patterns. Place a cake doily (the thicker the better, or two stuck together) on the crepe paper. Wearing rubber gloves, dip a sponge into a solution of bleach and water as above, squeeze out the excess and then gently but quickly dab across the doilies, working into the cut-out areas, reloading the sponge with bleach if necessary. Remove the doilies and allow to dry.

For all these techniques when you have finished painting your designs, leave them to dry in a well-ventilated space. Sometimes the smell of bleach can still be quite strong even after the paper has dried, though it will fade after a couple of days, or you could hang the paper on the line to air.

HINT

• If you are lacking confidence, practise first. If you are unsure about painting a pattern freehand, very lightly draw out a pattern with a soft pencil before painting.

• Experiment with different paintbrush sizes. Remember, bleach spreads, so always choose a brush finer than the scale of your desired design.

CHEAP CHIC

F ROM HUMBLE newspaper to functional hessian (burlap), there is a vast wealth of cheap and stylish materials which can be used to create wonderfully chic wraps.

In addition to hessian try other cheap fabrics, such as ticking, calico, muslin and even felt. Instead of expensive wrapping paper save money by using plain brown paper and sugar paper or even newspaper. For those larger presents, rolls of wallpaper lining are ideal. Never throw away plain paper bags, as they are perfect for covering gifts that have awkward angles. If you don't want plain paper visit your local stationers and hunt out all sorts of office stickers then use these to decorate your wrappings. You could also use raffle tickets, airmail stickers and used stamps, roughly torn from their envelopes and stuck on at random. Sometimes it is easier to decorate the paper after wrapping the present.

Corrugated card rolled into tubes is ideal for disguising presents such as money or tokens. If you make your own curtains, left-over scraps of gathered or pencil–pleat heading tape pulled up and tied round these tubes of corrugated card look very effective. Other scraps of material which are equally effective are pieces of needlepoint canvas. A 7.5cm (3in) strip of canvas wrapped around a present, the ends secured with double-sided tape and the sides frayed, looks very stylish.

In addition to using string and raffia to tie up your gifts, use it to make stylish tassels (see pg 68-69). Other finishing touches include paper ribbon, dried leaves, seed pods and cones. Or try wrapping small empty match boxes or stock cubes in brown paper; tie them with string or gold thread, then attach them to the parcel. And never forget the classic luggage label.

If you have the use of a photocopier, you could copy and enlarge areas from a newspaper. Crosswords are particularly good when scaled up. Always remember that wrapping gifts should be fun – the simplest ideas which make elegant use of original materials are often the most effective.

STYLISH BOTTLES

RUMMAGE THROUGH all those fabric remnants you could never bring yourself to throw away, add a few sheets of tissue paper, roll out the ribbon and with a quick snip with the pinking shears nothing could be easier than wrapping a bottle with style.

MATERIALS

Fabric remnants
Tissue paper
Double-sided tape
Plain paper for labels
Ribbon
String
Pinking shears (optional)

Tissue paper, crepe paper and fabric remnants are ideal for wrapping bottles. Not only are they widely available in a multitude of glorious colours, but they also give a neat finish.

Cutting the edges with pinking shears gives an attractive effect that also prevents fraying. For loosely woven fabrics like hessian (burlap), fray the edges rather than using pinking shears.

Instead of ribbon and string, finish the wrapped bottle with a raffia bow and tassels to match (see pg 68-69), feathers or dried leaves sprayed with gold paint, Christmas baubles, or a twist of ivy.

Soak a label off an empty wine or beer bottle and use it as a label. It will look wonderful with neutral-coloured fabrics like muslin and hessian, or dramatic with black crepe paper.

Smaller, more feminine gifts such as perfume can be wrapped in small-scale gingham and finished with wide lace.

TO COVER A BOTTLE COMPLETELY

1 Cut the paper or fabric. For the width cut the paper a little wide than the bottle's circumference. Allow for extra length at each end of the gift, adding enough at the base to cover half the bottle's diameter, and at the top adding an extra 7 – 12cm (3 – 5in), depending on the size of the bottle.

2 Roll the paper around the bottle and secure with tape. Pleat the base neatly as for wrapping a cylinder (see pg 14). Secure all the folds with tape.

3 Stand the bottle up and fold down the paper at the top of the bottle, folding two or three times towards the back. Secure with double-sided tape.

4 To finish, tie string, ribbon or fabric around the neck. Wrap contrasting paper or fabric around the centre if desired.

5 Attach a label (made from paper or fabric, possibly with pinked edges) to the front of the bottle with glue or double-sided tape.

TO COVER A BOTTLE, LEAVING THE TOP OPEN

1 Cut the main fabric as directed for covering a bottle completely, but do not add any extra length at the top. Cut contrasting fabric the same width as the main fabric but only half the length of the bottle.

2 Place the pieces of fabric together, wrong sides up, allowing the contrasting fabric to overlap the main fabric by 2.5 – 5cm (1 – 2in) as shown *(below)*. Secure the side and bottom with double-sided tape. Tie at the neck before turning the contrasting fabric to the right side.

STENCILLED IVY

LET IVY LEAVES RUN RIOT across your gifts, by making your own exclusive hand-painted paper, using simple stencils. Combined with pretty ribbons and artifical flowers, it looks colourful and fresh.

Stencilling, like stamping and potato printing, is one of the fastest ways to transform plain paper. You can either make your own stencil as shown here or buy one ready-made from the vast choice now available. Or you might already have some stencils you've used for decorating walls and furniture. Gather other simple-shaped leaves – oak leaves are perfect – and use as outlines for making your stencils.

MATERIALS

Tracing paper
Thin card
Cutting mat or thick cardboard
Craft knife or small pair of scissors
Gouache or acrylic paint
Sponge
Plain paper

1 Transfer the leaf outline given on page 109 onto a piece of tracing paper; or, for different-sized leaves, enlarge or reduce the design on a photocopier. Transfer the leaf onto the thin card, ensuring that the outline is clear. Carefully following the traced lines and working on a cutting mat or thick cardboard, accurately cut out the shape using a craft knife or a pair of small, sharp scissors.

2 Next, place some of the paint in a saucer, mixing colours if desired. You may need to add a drop of water if the paint is very thick, but avoid making it at all runny or the colour could smudge.

3 If you have never stencilled before, practise the technique first, working on a surface similar to the one you want to decorate. For best results, stencil on a flat, smooth surface. Hold the stencil firmly in place with one hand while you gently dab the colour on using the sponge with the other hand. Be careful not to load the sponge with too much paint, or colour will seep under the stencil. Any excess on the sponge should be blotted off on a piece of kitchen paper (paper towel).

4 Lift the stencil off quickly to avoid smudging the paint, and reposition it ready for the next leaf. There is no need to reload the sponge with paint after each leaf – you can work until the sponge is almost dry. The variation in colour density adds interest. For the same reason, vary the pressure with which you dab the sponge.

5 Apply the stencil either randomly across the paper or in a regular pattern such as rows. For the latter it is a good idea to mark out the position of the leaves with a soft pencil before stencilling.

VARIATIONS

• Invent your own stencil patterns, remembering that the cut-out area must not be too intricate or extensive, or the stencil will disintegrate.

• If you are planning to use your stencil repeatedly, it is worth coating it with varnish to make it both tougher and waterproof. Alternatively, you can cut your stencil out of a sheet of oiled stencil card or acetate. Acetate does have the advantage of allowing you to see exactly where you are stencilling, but it is harder to cut. Making a long-lasting stencil will enable you to use it for stencilling not just paper, but also fabric, accessories and even walls.

• The photograph shows a coloured stencil on white, but colour on colour looks equally effective. Black or white on traditional brown paper, or red on blue also looks great.

• For tags and cards, place the stencil in the centre of a piece of card and dab the shape with glue. Remove the stencil and cover the glue with gold glitter.

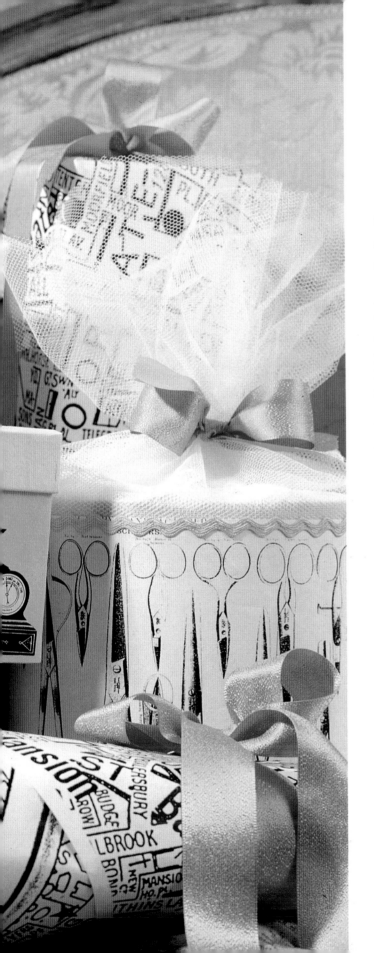

BLOW UP

ONE OF THE EASIEST ways to create your own wrapping paper is to use enlarged photocopied images. It is also extremely versatile, being suitable for all occasions – including birthdays, weddings, anniversaries and Christmas.

Almost anything can be made into an interesting image for wrapping paper. Try enlarging an image repeatedly. Books and catalogues, illustrated with black-and-white engravings rather than photographs, offer a superb source of images to copy. In particular, look for old illustrated encyclopedias and pictorial reference books, full of copyright-free designs and motifs.

If possible, choose pictures that relate to the recipient of the gift or to the occasion. For example, for a housewarming, as shown here, choose images associated with the home, such as clocks, cutlery, china or street maps.

In addition to using images from books you could also copy and enlarge bits of newspaper – crosswords are particularly good – as well as maps, musical scores (see pages 24-5) and even lace.

Either use the photocopied paper whole, taping pieces together to make a larger piece if necessary, or cut out the images and stick them onto coloured paper as for découpage (see pages 64-5). If you prefer you can first wrap a present in plain paper, or tissue and lace, and then wrap a piece of photocopied paper just around the main part of the gift.

If you can't find anything suitable, you could create your own images and patterns to copy. Try sticking used stamps randomly onto a sheet of plain paper, even overlapping some of them, and then copying and enlarging this again and again until you have the pattern as large as you wish. (Keep your original sheet of stamps in a safe place for later wrappings.) Or instead of stamps, follow the same technique but use playing cards, old business cards, raffle tickets, airmail stickers and even photographs.

TARTAN BOXES

BRING A SENSE of the Scottish
Highlands to your gift wraps
with a tartan-patterned gift box. If
you can't find a tartan fabric or paper,
cover the box in a plain-coloured
paper, choosing one of the classic
tartan colours like red, deep blue or
pine green, and trim or tie it with a
tartan ribbon. One idea for using
tartan is shown opposite, and many
more on pages 46-7.

A box is needed in order to do justice to
the graphic plaid pattern. You can, of
course, use an existing box, but it is not
difficult to make one yourself, and it is
particularly useful for gifts that are an
awkward shape. Indeed, a beautifully
made box is a gift in itself. Instructions
are given here for actually making a gift
box. For how to cover it, see pages 102-3.

MATERIALS

Thick card
Pencil
Metal ruler
Craft knife
Set square
Cutting board
Plastic parcel tape

1 Carefully measure out and draw
the shape of the box on the card,
using the template on page 106.
(To make a larger or smaller box,
simply scale up or down each
measurement.) Use your set square for
the right angles.

2 Cut out the shape with a sharp
craft knife, working on a cutting
mat or thick cardboard and using
the ruler as a guide.

3 Score along the dotted lines
shown on the template using the
back of a craft knife or the blunt
edge of a pair of scissors.
Carefully fold the card along the score
lines. Make sure each fold line is well
creased, to give a crisp shape. Hold the
sides together, inside and out, with parcel
tape *(below)*.

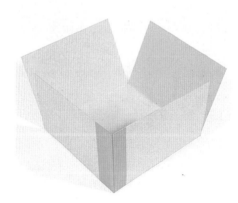

4 To make the lid, first measure
out on card a square 8mm
(1¼ in) larger each way than the
base of the box. Add sides 2.5cm
(1in) deep. Cut out and assemble the lid
in the same way as the box.

VARIATIONS

• A lovely way of giving a posy of flowers
is to place it in a box that has been
covered in fabric or paper which
complements the hues of the flowers.
Long after the flowers have wilted and
died, the box remains a memento of the
occasion, be it Mother's Day, anniversary
or whatever. To protect a box of flowers
in transit, gently scrunch up some tissue
paper and line the box with it. This will
support the posy.

• Your tartan-covered box doesn't have to
be square or rectangular. It could equally
well be cylindrical. A cylindrical box looks
much more difficult to make than it is. To
work out the measurement of the box,
first wrap a piece of paper around the gift.
Cut it to the correct width and height,
and use as a template to cut out a piece of
cardboard. Roll the cardboard into a
cylinder and hold the two ends together
with parcel tape. (Do not overlap the
edges or you will get a ridge.) Draw and
cut out a circular base and attach with
small pieces of tape. For the lid, cut out a
slightly larger circle, and for the lid sides
cut out a piece of cardboard that is
slightly longer than the circumference of
the cylinder. Stick the edge of the strip to
the edge of the circle with small pieces
of the parcel tape.

BUNDLES OF INTRIGUE

AN IDEAL USE for remnants of beautiful fabrics – from silk and velvet to cotton and lace – is to wrap them around your gifts. If you are not a hoarder of fabric scraps, interior decorating shops and upholsterers are worth trying for pretty fabrics. They often give away, or sell very cheaply, fabric samples and even old sample books. It is also always worth watching out for interesting cheap fabrics, particularly if you want to wrap a large gift or make a giant fabric bow.

MATERIALS

Scraps of fabric
Elastic bands (rubber bands)
Pinking shears
Ribbon
Double-sided tape
Large buttons

1 To wrap a small, awkward shape with pretty fabric, use pinking shears to cut a circle of fabric at least 2-2¹/2 times bigger than the gift. (If necessary, use a round object as a template.) It is better to cut the fabric too large than too small, as any excess can be cut off later. If the gift needs padding to protect it, wrap a sheet of tissue paper or bubble wrap around it. Place the gift in the middle of the cloth and either bunch or pleat the fabric over it. Secure with an elastic band (rubber band). Finish with a length of ribbon tied into a bow.

2 To wrap a tubular present or a rolled-up soft gift (for example, a scarf), use pinking shears to cut a piece of fabric at least 13cm (5in) wider than the gift and long enough to roll around the object with some overlap. Place the gift in the middle of the fabric and roll it up, sticking down the overlap with double-sided tape. Bunch up each end and secure with an elastic band (rubber band). Cover each band with a ribbon tied into a bow.

3 To wrap a flat, regular-shaped object, use pinking shears to cut a piece of fabric nearly twice the length of the gift and wide enough to wrap around the object with some overlap. Place the gift in the centre of the fabric and wrap the fabric around it. Stick the fabric down with double-sided tape, making sure the join line follows the centre of the object. Either fold the end flaps in towards the middle or fold each flap into a point before folding it in towards the centre. For both methods, stick down the flaps with double-sided tape or cut a strip of fabric and wrap it around the gift, securing it with tape in the centre. Decorate with large buttons held in position with double-sided tape.

VARIATION

• For special presents, make simple 'couture' bags (see pages 33 and 68) from remnants of luxury fabrics like velvet, silk, satin and shimmering gauze. Fabric bags are very simple to make, especially if you have a sewing machine. For each bag, cut out two rectangular pieces of fabric of the same size. With right sides facing, pin and sew them together – either by hand using backstitch, or by machine – around two long and one short side, taking at least a 1cm (³/8in) seam allowance. Clip the seam allowances diagonally across the two bottom corners. Turn the bag right side out and hem the top edge. To close, simply gather up the top of the bag near the opening and tie with cord or ribbon. Decorate the bags with offcuts of braid, tassels (see pages 68-9), ribbons, beads and buttons as well as ribbon roses (see pages 32-3 and 62-3).

RIBBON ROSETTES

FOR THE SMARTEST, most elegant pile of presents, adorn each gift with a cluster of red ribbon rosettes.

Rosettes are made from a continuous length of ribbon which is folded repeatedly at right angles until there are several layers of folds, forming 'petals'. The size of the rosette will depend on the number of folds as well as the width of ribbon used. Small rosettes made out of 1.2-–2.5cm ($^1/_2$–1in) wide ribbon need no more than four layers of folds. For a large, more extravagant rosette made out of wider ribbon there may be as many as eight layers of folds.

When making ribbon rosettes, it is important to use the correct ribbon. Most ribbons with a matt finish are suitable. Taffeta makes wonderful rosettes – try not just the plain colours but also the plaids, checks and stripes. For a very different effect, cotton seam binding works well; it is particularly easy to use as it doesn't slip during folding. Also try single-face satin, a satin ribbon that is shiny on one side and matt on the other side. Wired and grosgrain ribbons are to be avoided.

MATERIALS

2.5cm (1in) wide red ribbon
Matching sewing thread
Double-sided tape or glue

1 Cut a length of ribbon 45cm (18in) long and lay it horizontally on a flat surface. Starting 5cm (2in) from the right-hand end, fold the ribbon over at a 90-degree angle. Following the step photograph *(below)*, continue to fold the ribbon in this way, until four layers of folded ribbon have been made, with four folds per layer.

2 Very carefully pass the tail end of the ribbon through the centre of the rosettes to the other side *(above right)*. Gently pull until the top layer of folds starts to spiral tightly in the centre. Do not pull too much through or you will start to unravel all the folds. Pinch the two ends together and with, matching sewing thread, make a couple of stitches to secure. Cut off the excess ribbon.

3 If you wish your rosette to have tails, use a longer piece of ribbon. Start the first fold at least 10cm (4in) from one edge. After completing the rosette do not trim the ends but allow them to dangle below the rosette.

4 Secure the rosettes to your gifts using double-sided tape or glue. Arrange them singly, in rows or in clusters.

VARIATION

• A bold black-and-white coat button makes a dramatic base on which to glue three rosettes together. Choose a button larger than the rosettes and in a contrasting colour or pattern, and this will frame them beautifully. Use it as the centrepiece for your gift wrapping.

BUTTERFLY BONANZA

DRAW INSPIRATION from a summer garden and use découpage techniques to decorate your gifts with fluttering butterflies or other colourful images.

Découpage is the art of decorating a surface using paper cut-outs. Traditionally many layers of varnish are used to give a smooth surface and make the cut-outs look like hand-painting, but it is not necessary to go to those lengths for gift wraps.

Magazines, greetings cards, even seed packets and plant catalogues all provide suitable images. Alternatively, you can obtain colour photocopies of book illustrations. For maximum impact, it's a good idea to work to a theme, such as the butterflies used here.

There's no need to use only colour images. Black-and-white cut-outs can look very dramatic, especially on coloured paper (see pages 78-9).

MATERIALS

Butterfly prints
Paper glue
Small sharp scissors

For wrapping gifts

Brightly coloured paper
Cellophane

For decorating gift boxes

Black paint and fine paintbrush, or fine black marker (optional)
Clear varnish
Paintbrush, for varnishing

WRAPPING GIFTS

1 Neatly wrap your gift in coloured paper. Fresh, bright colours, reminiscent of summer flowers, are ideal for a butterfly theme, or you might wish to use softer colours to match butterflies in delicate shades of blue and pink.

2 Using small, sharp scissors, cut out each butterfly motif. The antennae are much too fiddly to cut around, so trim these off – you can always paint them in later. Apply a thin layer of glue or spray adhesive to the wrong side of the cut-outs and stick them on at random or in a pattern. Press down firmly.

3 Wrap the present in cellophane in the same way as you do paper, but folding only one end. Gather up the other end and secure with ribbon or string.

DECORATING A GIFT BOX

1 Prepare the box to be decorated, painting or covering it with coloured paper (see pages 102-3). Cut out and apply the butterflies as for step 2, left. After gluing, smooth all the butterflies flat, making sure there are no air bubbles.

2 If you wish, paint in the butterflies' antennae using a small paintbrush and black paint, or draw them in using a fine black marker. Allow to dry.

3 Apply the varnish with a paintbrush. Do not varnish too thickly or it will cause drips. Unlike traditional découpage, there is no need to apply more than one coat of varnish.

4 To finish the edge, you could, if desired, glue ribbon trim all around the rim of the box, as shown in the photograph.

VARIATION

• A lovely way of using butterfly cut-outs is to stick them onto the cellophane wrapped around a bouquet of flowers. Arrange them randomly at the top of the bouquet (you don't need many) and it will look as though you have butterflies fluttering around your flowers.

AWKWARD SHAPES

WRAPPING AWKWARD shapes can be demoralizing. However hard you try, the gift ends up looking a mess, with the wrapping paper creased and untidy. It is not only the awkward angles that are difficult – sometimes the sheer size of the gift makes it seem particularly daunting.

But it is a shame not to wrap presents, however awkward or large. It is the unwrapping of a gift, the tearing of the paper, that is always so exciting, particularly for children. See the wrapping as an exciting challenge, one in which you can have a lot of fun.

The solution is not to be too precious about the task. You are not aiming for a crease-free wrap but for a gift that looks colourful and witty. Instead of buying expensive wrapping paper, use sheets of newspaper, or rolls of brown paper or wallpaper – both lining paper and the patterned type. Look out for ends of lines (odd rolls can frequently be picked up for next to nothing) as well as wallpaper sample books.

The sheets can be taped together to create a wrapping paper that has a wonderful patchwork effect. This effect can also be achieved by taping pages from colourful magazines, catalogues or comics together.

The gift shown here is a tricycle for a child's third birthday, with ears and a tail added to make it look less obvious. Many large objects can be wrapped in this way, such as a wheelbarrow (perhaps covered in pages from an old glossy flower catalogue), a piano stool (wrapped in a photocopied music score) or a large ornate mirror (in pages from a glossy fashion magazine). Small awkward shapes can be wrapped in fabric (see pages 60-1) or cellophane.

MATERIALS

For large awkward shapes

Old children's comics
Double sided-tape
Piece of lightweight cardboard
Coloured card for tag

For small awkward shapes

Brightly coloured cellophane
String
Ribbon

LARGE AWKWARD SHAPES

1 Starting with the main part of the bike, loosely wrap comic pages around it, securing the pages together with just the odd piece of double-sided tape here and there. If a piece of paper is too large or is not the right shape, don't hesitate to do some cutting and trimming. If you cut too much off, just add another piece.

2 After wrapping the main part of the bike, cover the wheels. Make little envelopes to cover the pedals. Roll pages, as though you were wrapping a bouquet of flowers, to form ear-like shapes in which to cover the handlebars.

3 For the tail, roll up a piece of lightweight cardboard (if it is too heavy, it will not stand up) and cover with more comic. Roll a double sheet from the magazine and tape it at one end. Cut the rest of it into strips to form a tail end. Secure to the cardboard tube with more tape.

4 Cut a shaped tag out of coloured card. You could use a number to indicate a child's birthday, or instead of a number make a tag out of the initial of the recipient.

SMALL AWKWARD SHAPES

1 For these, use brightly coloured cellophane rather than paper. Cut a square or circle of cellophane two or three times bigger than the object.

2 Gather the cellophane up and tie it into a bunch above the present. Secure with string. Cover the string with a ribbon tied into a bow, or any other trimming.

RAFFIA TASSELS

EVEN THE SIMPLEST of hand-tied tassels will add opulence to your gifts. They are incredibly easy and quick to make. They are also addictive – before you know it you will have made hundreds of them and saved yourself a fortune!

Tassels can be made from all sorts of materials, including string, knitting yarn (look out for sparkling Lurex), embroidery thread, even fine ribbons. In order to create a contrast of textures with the silk bags (see page 61 for how to make them), the tassels shown here have been made from raffia, which now is available in a wonderful assortment of attractive colours.

MATERIALS

Cardboard
Raffia
Strong gold thread or yarn
Large decorative buttons (optional)
Cord (optional)

1 Cut a piece of cardboard, and wind the raffia around it. The length of the tassels will depend on the depth of the piece of cardboard, and their thickness on how many times you wind the yarn around it – the more yarn you use, the fuller the tassel will be.

2 Thread a length of gold yarn or thread through all the strands and tie the yarn or thread firmly at the top of the cardboard as shown, leaving the ends long *(below, left)*. Cut through the strands of yarn at the opposite end of the tie.

3 To finish, wind another piece of gold yarn three or four times around the tassel, about 1cm (³/8in) from the top, and knot firmly *(below, right)*. Trim the ends, tucking any excess underneath. If some of the raffia threads are too thick, split them using a needle.

4 Secure the tassels to your gifts or silk gift bags using the gold ends at the top of each tassel, adding large decorative buttons and cord if desired *(above right)*.

VARIATIONS

• For a multi-coloured tassel, combine two or more coloured threads or materials. Work in exactly the same way as for a small tassel, but wind the coloured threads together around the cardboard.

• If you are dyeing some fabrics or clothes, why not quickly make an assortment of tassels out of household cotton string, and throw these into the dye as well? It's always worth having a few spare pretty-coloured tassels.

• On page 101, a hessian (burlap) lined gift basket has been decorated with dried orange slices. You could replace these with generous tassels made out of raffia to complement the hessian. Make them all in one colour, or alternate different colours around the basket.

TRIM PLEATS

ELEGANT AND TAILORED, this gift wrap technique could be called the couture-ladies look. But unlike couture, it costs next to nothing to achieve. All you need are a sophisticated colour theme, neat wrapping and some crisp touches of pleating.

Pleated paper also can be used to wrap around a simple posy of fresh or dried flowers. With a ribbon tied around the base, the effect is charming *(left)*.

MATERIALS

Lilac-coloured paper
4cm (1/2in) wide navy velvet ribbon
Double-sided tape
White paper
1cm (3/8in) wide lilac ribbon
7.5cm (3in) wide lilac ribbon
Florist wire
Small piece of thin white ribbon

LILAC PARCEL

1 Wrap a gift in lilac paper. Wrap a length of navy velvet ribbon lengthwise around the centre of the parcel, and secure it at the base with double-sided tape.

2 To make a length of pleated paper ribbon, cut a piece of the white paper 2.5cm (1in) wide. Cut the strip as long as possible, sticking two pieces together if necessary. Along one edge mark with a pencil every 5cm (2in).

3 Working on a flat surface, lay the strip of paper horizontally. At the first pencil mark on the left-hand side, fold the paper at 90 degrees towards you. At the second pencil mark, fold it at 90 degrees again but this time folding it under and passing the paper to the right. Repeat this sequence until you have enough pleated paper. Crease each fold well using your thumbnail. To save time you might only want to pleat enough to cross the top and sides of your gift.

4 Wrap around the present and secure at the base with tape. Cut off any excess paper. Carefully weave a length of narrow lilac ribbon through the paper pleats and secure it at the base with double-sided tape.

WHITE PARCELS

1 Wrap a gift in white paper. Measure the length of the top and multiply by three. Add this measurement to the total length of the three remaining sides, plus a little for overlap. This is how much wide lilac ribbon you will need.

2 Pleat the centre of the wide lilac ribbon with 2.5cm (1in) box pleats. It should not be creased too firmly.

3 Secure the pleats in position with double-sided tape. Wrap around the gift then finish with the striped ribbon on top. Secure at the base with double-sided tape.

4 To make a fan, see page 24. Hold the pleated paper closed while you tie a piece of florist wire around the centre. Gently fan out the paper until it forms nearly a full circle of pleats. Cover the wire with a thin piece of white ribbon tied into a bow. Attach the fan to the present with double-sided tape.

VARIATION

• Substitute fabric for the striped ribbon, cutting the fabric with pinking shears to prevent fraying. Or simply use coloured paper cut into strips.

AUTUMNAL TRIMMINGS

GATHER THE TREASURES of autumn, when the landscape is a blaze of russets, reds, golds, oranges and browns, and adorn your gifts with these glorious colours and textures all year round.

In the autumn, make the most of a country walk and gather up leaves in all shapes, sizes and colours. They look wonderful with rustic materials like raffia, string, terracotta and hessian (burlap) as well as with traditional brown paper and corrugated card. Watch out too for small twigs, fir cones, seedheads and spiky grains and grasses. They are stunning with leaves or on their own. Little posies of dried flowers such as roses, lavender or hydrangea florets can be used in a similar way. With this little bit of forward planning, you can have a supply of autumnal trimmings for decorating wrapped presents and gift baskets throughout the year.

Freshly fallen leaves are surprisingly strong and pliable, so in addition to trimming presents with them, you could use them to decorate clay flowerpots to hold small gifts. Make sure the leaves are completely dry, then apply a thin layer of PVA adhesive (white glue). Allow the glue to become tacky before pressing the leaves into position. Stick a row of leaves around the side of the pot, overlapping each one slightly, then finish with a raffia bow.

Or, if you prefer, cover a whole box, such as a wooden cheese box, overlapping the leaves until the background colour no longer shows. To stop the leaves from curling at the edges while the glue is drying, use weights on the top and clothes pegs (clothespins) or bulldog clips on the sides (protecting the leaves with paper). When the box is dry, paint on a thin layer of clear varnish.

Another idea is to wrap freshly fallen leaves (before they have time to dry out) around the stems of a small posy of flowers, securing them with a raffia bow. For simple cards and tags, cut out plain card and glue on just one beautiful leaf in the centre.

POTATO PRINTS

JUST AS VERSATILE in printing as it is in cooking, the humble potato offers instant success with your gift wraps.

Using a potato to create bold and beautiful designs couldn't be simpler. There are no special skills required, it costs almost nothing to do and a sheet of paper can be decorated in seconds.

Always work on a flat, smooth surface and print onto a porous paper – avoid paper with a glossy sheen. The larger the potato, the better, as it will give you more area to design with.

The most successful designs are usually the simplest. Here three different motifs are used: a circle, a cross and a moon. Other possible designs which are suitable for potato printing include squares, stripes and chevrons.

MATERIALS

Large potato
Sharp knife
Gouache or poster paint
Matt paper
Soft pencil
Paintbrush

1 Cut a large potato in half and rinse it under a cold tap to remove any starch residue. Allow it to dry, then, with a pencil, draw a simple design on the cut surface of the potato.

2 Using a sharp knife, cut away the part of the potato surrounding the design, leaving the design itself raised from the surface.

3 In an old saucer or shallow container, mix up the poster paint or gouache to the required colour, being careful not to make it too thin, or smudging during printing will occur.

4 Before printing, if you are unsure about using the stamp freehand, mark out the position of the motifs on the paper with a soft pencil. This is also a good idea if you want the motifs printed in a particular pattern.

5 Use a paintbrush to apply the paint evenly and not too thickly to the potato stamp. Press the stamp down firmly onto the paper and lift it off with a steady hand.

6 For an evenly coloured design, recoat the potato with paint before each impression. Or, to vary the amount of colour, continue to use the potato until the colour has almost faded, and only then recoat the surface with paint. Allow the paint to dry thoroughly before using the paper.

VARIATIONS

• Instead of covering a whole piece of paper with just one motif, you could use two or even three different potato stamps on the same sheet. Either apply them randomly or create a repeating pattern. For example, you could alternate circles and crosses either in rows or in a grid pattern.

• You could also combine different colours. The papers shown here employ only blue on white and white on blue, but employing several colours on one sheet of paper is also effective. If you are using just one potato stamp, wash the potato clean and allow it to dry before applying the next colour. If you are covering a lot of paper, cut out a potato stamp for each colour.

• In addition to using potato stamps on paper, use them with fabric dyes to decorate cloth, which then could be used to wrap bottles (see pages 52-3) or to decorate gift baskets and jam jars.

• A very cheap and effective way to make a large quantity of patterned ribbon for extra-large presents is to cut strips of fabric 7.5–10cm (3–4in) wide with pinking shears and then print a pattern along the length of each strip.

FLORAL WRAPS

BREAK FROM CONVENTIONAL cellophane and delight everyone by giving posies and bouquets wrapped with ingenuity and originality.

When you give someone a bouquet of flowers, however small or grand, a little extra time and thought spent on the presentation will greatly enhance the gift. It doesn't need to be elaborate or time-consuming: a wonderful bow (see pages 16-21) may be all that's needed. Simple ideas are the most effective. A piece of tissue paper pleated, then wrapped and secured around a bunch of flowers so the pleats fan out, could not be easier.

With a long-stemmed bunch of flowers, you can hide the stems with corrugated card. Cut a piece wide enough to wrap around the stems and to overlap at the back, secure it with double-sided tape and finish with a bow. Brightly coloured flowers presented in this way look like flame torches.

For a fun 'welcome to your new home' posy, photocopy and enlarge the part of the map or street guide in which the new home is located and use this to wrap up the flowers. Black-and-white photocopies look particularly wonderful with deep red flowers and a big red bow.

Net is perfect for wrapping flowers. Big frothy summer blooms look particularly good wrapped in this way. Like cellophane, net holds its shape and frames a bunch of flowers beautifully. But unlike cellophane it comes in a multitude of colours, from the softest of pastels to the deepest of blues. To finish, cut a long narrow piece of net and wind it repeatedly around the stems before tying the ends.

Once a bunch of flowers is wrapped, the finishing touch is often to add a bow. Instead of ribbon, you can ring the changes by using sea-grass rope, string or raffia. In the autumn, substitute freshly fallen leaves that are still soft enough to tie around the stems. Another idea is to wind a piece of ivy around the stems of the flowers instead of a bow.

SILHOUETTES

F OR A WITTY GIFT BOX and a splash of colour, charmingly old-fashioned silhouettes are the answer. Though often associated with book illustrations and framed pictures, silhouettes lend themselves just as well to greetings cards, wrapping paper and decorated boxes.

To decorate a hat or gift box with silhouettes, first cover the box with coloured paper. Using the template on page 105, and enlarging or reducing it as required, transfer the silhouette onto white paper and the oval frame onto black paper. With small, sharp scissors, cut out both shapes, then glue the silhouette onto the black paper, making sure it is positioned centrally. Repeat until you have the required number of silhouettes. With a pencil, mark out on the box the position of each silhouette, then glue them onto the box.

Decorate the lid of the box with a large bow, made out of the same black and white paper that you have used for the silhouettes. Cut six strips of black paper 2.5cm (1in) wide, each as long as the diameter of the circular box. Cut six strips of white to match. Fold each strip in half, but do not crease the folds. With glue, secure the two ends together, forming loops. Alternating black and white, arrange the loops in the centre of the lid, overlapping each one and spacing them evenly. Hold them in position with either glue or tape. Finish the centre of the bow with a circle of black paper, topped with a large gilt button.

To make a silhouette greetings card, fold a piece of white cardboard in half, and glue a rectangle of coloured paper onto it, leaving a white border all around. Prepare a silhouette in the same way as for the boxes and glue it to the centre of the coloured paper. If desired, decorate with a bow.

If you find the combination of black and white with bright pink too vivid, try other colour combinations, such as cream silhouettes framed in lilac and placed on navy, or gold silhouettes framed in white and placed on red or brown paper.

TOP DRESSING

YOU HAVE SPENT HOURS making delicious marmalade, so why not spend a few moments more making your own unique jar tops? They will make the gift of home-made preserves even more special.

MATERIALS

For printed jar tops

Compass
String
Thick cardboard
Orange artist's gouache or acrylic paint
White paper
Wide paintbrush

For bleached jar tops

Yellow and orange crepe paper
Masking tape
Compass
Household bleach
Small paintbrush
Pinking shears or scissors
Elastic bands (rubber bands)
Raffia, cord or ribbon
Slices of dried orange (optional)

The colours of the paper and paint used here are suitable for orange marmalade. For other marmalades, jams, preserves and chutneys, use these two techniques but alter the colour of the paper or paint to match the ingredients – for example, green for gooseberry, black for blackberry and red for cherry jam. Using the bleaching technique, try other patterns – for example, tiny dashes that look like seeds.

PRINTED JAR TOPS

1 Using a compass draw a 15cm (6in) diameter circle onto the cardboard. In the centre of this circle draw another circle, 2.5cm (1in) in diameter. Carefully cut around the larger circle and then remove the smaller circle from the centre so you have a hole.

2 As though you were making a pompom, wind a long piece of string evenly through the hole again and again. Continue winding around the circular rim until you are back to where you started. When you have finished, the string should radiate from the centre so the cardboard looks like a cross-section of an orange. Secure both ends of the string with tape on one side only (which will be the wrong side).

3 Mix your paint in a saucer, being careful not to make the colour too liquid or it will smudge. Using a large paintbrush, apply the paint to the right side of the cardboard until all the string is covered.

4 Using this as a stamp, press the painted string down firmly onto the paper and then lift it off with a steady hand. For best results, use the stamp on a flat, smooth surface. The stamp must be recoated with paint before each impression. Continue until you have printed enough circles. Allow to dry. Finish and decorate as for bleached jar tops (see below).

BLEACHED JAR TOPS

Use the technique of bleaching crepe paper (see page 48) to create these jar tops which look like cross-sections of oranges. Take some crepe paper and use a compass to draw on it circles large enough to cover the tops of the jars. Using bleach, paint lines radiating from the centre of each circle. When completely dry, cut out each circle with a pair of pinking shears or plain scissors, and stretch one across each jar top. Secure with an elastic band (rubber band) and decorate with raffia, orange cord, yellow ribbon, or a slice of dried orange held in place with double-sided tape or glue.

LABELS OF LOVE

GIFT TAGS ARE AN IMPORTANT part of a present, but so often a wrapped gift is spoiled by a message scrawled across its surface or a tag that is quite clearly an afterthought. Yet with just a little time, you can make a gift tag that will make your present look quite special. Even a present wrapped in cheap brown paper and tied with string can be made to look very smart.

Labels can match or contrast with the gift wrap. One of the easiest ways to make a unique tag is to start with a luggage label. You can either stick or paint things onto this, or cut into it. Choose the size of luggage label that best suits the size of your gift; large labels can always be cut down to size.

The simplest transformation of a luggage label is to draw a border in ink, or paint it, around the rim of the tag. It could be just one solid line or a row of tiny motifs such as crosses, hearts or diamonds. Thread the punched hole with ribbon or cord.

Offcuts of ribbon and other trimmings, such as braids, beads and sequins, can all be used to decorate a tag, as well as small remnants of brown needlepoint canvas and hessian with the edges frayed. Onto these you could add a line of buttons, a small shell or even a tassel made out of string (see pages 68-9). All sorts of unusual items can be used to adorn and uplift the humble luggage label, including cut-outs (see pages 64-5), odd playing cards, toy money, wired paper leaves used for cake decorating, dried leaves from the garden and even petals and slices of dried fruit.

A fun idea is to stick a used stamp onto one corner of a label and then wind and knot a piece of string around the label so that it looks like a wrapped parcel.

Instead of adding to a label, you can cut it to reflect a seasonal or thematic shape – for example, a heart for Valentine's Day or a house for a house-warming present.

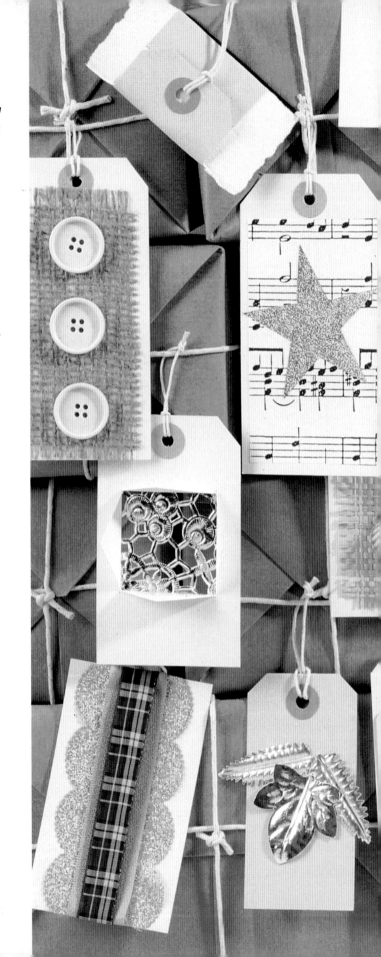

NOVELTY TAGS

IF YOU LOVE TO HOARD snippets of lace and ribbon, and odd bits of coloured paper, these gift tags will prove effortless to make.

In addition to luggage labels (see pages 82-3), gift tags can be based upon a variety of other materials. They can also be cut into shapes which echo the pattern or motif printed on the paper. A paper printed with gold stars requires no more than a simple star-shaped tag. Alternatively, you could cut out the shape of a star from the middle of a plain rectangular tag, to create a star-shaped window effect. Other tag shapes to try with your heavenly paper are the sun and moon.

Whatever shape you choose, it is important that the size of the tag contrasts with the size of the motif on the wrapping paper. One large, scaled-up star, for example, looks far more effective with lots of smaller printed stars, than if it were cut to the same size. If you are not sure what size to cut your tag, try different scales using scraps of paper before committing yourself.

For floral wraps, cut out different leaf shapes. If you are unsure about drawing the shape freehand, pick leaves from the garden and use these as templates to draw around. Textured hand-made paper is particularly suitable for leaf shapes. Other shapes that are good with floral papers are the shapes of garden tools – watering can, spade, bucket.

On a gift for someone who loves the seaside, or perhaps is spending a birthday there, naively shaped boats make perfect tags, as do starfish, shells, sea horses and fish.

The shape of tags can also be inspired by the season or occasion. Christmas is the most obvious – pine trees, stockings, angels all make good tags but there are many other possibilities, such as a key for a house-warming gift. For a child's birthday, use cookie cutters as templates for gingerbread men, pigs, hands, horses and other bold, childlike shapes.

Tags can reflect the personality or hobbies of a particular person too. For a cat lover you might make a cat-shaped tag; or for someone who is mad about Scottie dogs, a Scottie dog tag cut out of thin red or black cardboard with tartan ribbon bows around its neck. These look good added to a gift wrapped in tartan paper. For someone who enjoys tea, a teapot-shaped tag is fun; for a lover of opera, an opera mask; for someone keen on wildlife, a butterfly; or for a personalized tag, the initial of the recipient. This is a great success with children. Templates for a variety of shapes are on pages 104-105.

Whatever the shape of your tag, for it to be truly effective the colour should complement the paper. If you cannot find the correct colour of card, you can always glue coloured paper, however thin, onto card. The tags can then either be left plain or pieces of ribbon and lace can be used to turn them into something more luxurious.

Another idea for tags is to cut up empty seed packets (for vegetables as well as flowers), and stick the picture onto a piece of thin coloured card or thick paper. Paper cut-outs left over from découpage (see pages 64-5) can also be treated in this way.

If you have been bleaching patterns onto paper (see pages 48-9), why not cut out a few squares of different-coloured crepe paper, and with a fine paintbrush bleach out an initial? When the paper is dry, glue it onto a piece of contrasting cardboard.

Create lace-effect tags using paper doilies. Cut out a shape and stick this onto a piece of contrasting paper so that the lace pattern stands out. A white heart on black finished with a black-and-white checked bow looks very chic.

For a gift with a special message, make little envelopes to hold a small letter. Seal with sealing wax, a beautiful button or a tiny bow. You will probably discover that the best ideas often come after you have wrapped a gift and you are playing around with the remnants.

Boxes, Bags
and Baskets

ALL THE TRIMMINGS

WITH THE SIMPLEST of materials and the minimum of time and effort, you can transform bland gift baskets and wooden buckets into stylish gifts.

Small wooden buckets (available from delicatessens) similar to those on pages 96-7 were used, as well as circular French cheese boxes. The important thing is not to overdo the decoration. Resist the temptation of using too much. The ideas which are simplest and make elegant use of plain materials are often the most effective. Both the container and the trimmings should enhance each other. A small wooden Camembert box, painted white, looks far more dramatic with just one beautiful starfish on its lid, than if it were covered with a fussy design using lots of smaller shells.

When you are decorating the rim of a wooden bucket, choose shells of a similar size. Before gluing anything, work out how and where you want to arrange them. If the container is large or you are using a lot of shells, it helps to mark their positions with a pencil before starting.

Shells and rope used together are very effective. Tie a piece of rope twice around the rim of a container, and knot tightly. This should hold the rope in position. If it doesn't, paint a thin trail of glue around the rim and apply the rope on top of this. Hold with clothes pegs (clothespins) until dry. On top of the rope, glue shells spaced evenly apart.

Look out for shells with pre – drilled holes, especially long slender shells. Sew the shells onto plaited rope and tie it around the top of a gift basket, so the shells dangle down the side.

Or with thin cord or string tie just one perfect shell around the neck of a wrapped bottle or gift bag.

Often when you buy shells they come in net bags, and you can use these for small, awkward-shaped gifts. Line a container which is smaller than the bag with the rope netting, and then with a circle of muslin or plain cotton fabric, cutting the fabric two to three times bigger in diameter than your container. Place your gifts in the middle and gather up both the netting and fabric over them. Secure with rope. If you have a pre-drilled shell you could tie this on.

In addition to shells, there is a vast wealth of other materials which are equally effective for trimming gift baskets and boxes. A rummage through any haberdashery will unearth fantastic braids and trimmings. Tassels are always a success when it comes to decorating a gift basket. Make them out of coloured raffia (see pages 68-9). Don't limit yourself to one colour, but choose several and then alternate these around the top of a plain wooden bucket or a box covered in hessian. For feminine touches use lengths of pretty lace and ribbon (see pages 96-7).

Buttons can be used in the same way as shells. Glue a simple line of buttons around the rim of a gift basket, or along the lid rim of a fabric-covered box (see pages 102-3). If you have lots of tiny white buttons, paint a Camembert box black or navy and arrange the buttons into a simple pattern on the lid, such as the initial of the recipient.

Fresh leaves can be used (see pages 72-3) but if you want the decorated container to be a lasting gift, they are not suitable. Use instead dried seedheads, orange slices, cinnamon sticks, bay leaves, twigs, fir cones or leaves. These can either be used as they come for a rustic feel, or sprayed with gold paint (see pages 30-1) for a more regal look. And don't forget dried flower heads. Two or three flower heads tied together with a raffia bow couldn't be simpler, and they can look exquisite.

BAGS OF IDEAS

THE PERFECT SOLUTION for awkwardly shaped presents, gift bags not only are extremely quick and easy to make, but they can be made to any size.

You'll need a strong, good-quality paper for making bags. However, there's no need to rule out other paper since a thin paper can be glued over a thicker piece, using spray adhesive, before the bag is made. After gluing, make sure the paper is completely smooth. In this way newspaper and colourful pages from glossy magazines, and even something as delicate as tissue paper, can be used.

For Christmas, small bags made in seasonal colours and filled with tiny gifts or home-made sweets make charming tree decorations. You could possibly add pieces of winter greenery and berries to the front of each bag.

MATERIALS

Strong paper
Scissors
Glue or double-sided tape
Hole punch or thick needle
Cord or ribbon
Decorating materials such as buttons,
stamps, wine labels, cut-out images
from magazines

1 The dimensions of your finished bag will depend on what you choose to use as a 'mould'. One book, or several in a pile, are ideal. To make your bag, cut a piece of paper long enough to wrap around your mould, adding an extra 2.5cm (1in) for overlapping. Fold over the top edge of the bag as shown *(below)*.

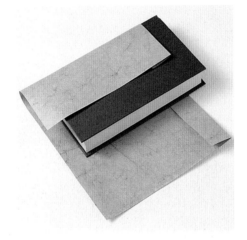

2 Wrap the paper neatly around your mould. Secure the overlap at the back with either glue or double-sided tape. To make the base of the bag, fold over the end flaps as for wrapping any regular-shaped present, creasing each fold firmly *(above right)*. Secure with plenty of glue or tape.

3 Remove the mould. Gently fold in the sides of the bag, creasing them in half at the top. Fold the base up over the back of the bag. Using either a hole punch or a thick needle, make one or two holes at the top of the bag on each side. Thread the bag with cord or ribbon, and decorate if required *(below)*.

SWEET BOXES AND CONES

K EEP FAMILY AND FRIENDS SWEET with these delightfully old-fashioned boxes and cones, overflowing with sugared almonds or other sweets (candies).

SWEET BOXES

Photocopy the two templates shown on page 107, enlarging them to the required size. Make sure you enlarge each shape by the same amount. Carefully cut them out.

Next prepare your wallpaper. With a non-toxic paper glue, glue a piece of patterned wallpaper (large enough to fit the templates) onto a sheet of contrasting wallpaper. Remnants of floral and striped wallpaper work well with toning plain papers. Smooth out any bubbles and allow to dry.

Trace the templates onto the prepared paper. Cut out and score along the dotted lines, using the blunt side of a pair of scissors. Fold along the score lines to make a box. Glue the side flap to the inside of the opposite edge. Glue the bottom flaps to the outside base and the inside base down to hide the bottom flaps. Fill with treats and fold down the flaps. Secure with a ribbon.

SWEET CONES

For the outside of the cone, cut a piece of patterned wallpaper 15cm (6in) square. For the inside, cut a piece in a contrasting paper adding 1cm (3/8in) to two dimensions. Cover the smaller piece with PVA adhesive (white glue) and stick it to the larger piece, carefully aligning two adjacent edges. Seen from the right side, this will give you a border along the other two edges.

Holding the lined paper in the shape of a diamond and with the border edges at the top, roll the other two edges towards each other, until they overlap at the top and meet at the bottom to form a point. Secure with double-sided tape. Add a small bow.

CULINARY GIFT BASKETS

TO WRAP GIFTS for foodies, you need look no further than the kitchen shop for a wealth of wonderful tin containers in which to offer your gifts.

Quiche, bread and pie tins all come in a variety of sizes. Line these with pretty fabric remnants, lace-trimmed handkerchiefs or napkins, letting the fabric fall out over the rim. Pad with coloured tissue paper. Into these you might like to place petits-fours, teas, sugared fruits, chutneys, relishes, sauces, spices, and jams.

When you have arranged your presents in the container, wrap the whole gift in clear cellophane. Cut a piece of cellophane at least 2–2$^{1}/_{2}$ times bigger than the gift. Place the gift in the centre, and bunch the cellophane up over it. Secure with an elastic band (rubber band) and finish with a ribbon, cord, or raffia bow.

Patty tins look wonderful filled with individually wrapped gifts, such as home-made truffles and marzipan sweets which could be offered at the end of a dinner party. Tin buckets are the perfect containers for bottles. To decorate them, cut a length of net long enough to tie around the rim of the bucket and into a knot or bow at the front. If necessary, hold it in place by winding a piece of florist wire around the net in two places (next to the bow and at the opposite end), taping the wire end to the inside of the bucket. Tease out the net so that it looks more like swags. You might wish to finish with more decoration – tassels, buttons, ribbon roses – or with something that fits in with the theme of the gift. For the bucket of three different olive oils shown here, for example, a couple of garlic bulbs have been used.

For something wacky, presents can be hidden in containers. Try placing a gift in a bowl which you then turn upside down and wrap in muslin. Place this in a colander and finish with thick string knotted through the holes. Gather the string at the top with a froth of muslin, a circle of chillies and a bulb of garlic.

BERIBBONED BUCKETS

SMALL WOODEN BUCKETS from delicatessens make wonderful containers for gifts, particularly for a themed collection of small presents such as toiletries.

MATERIALS

For gift bucket with soaps and candle
Wooden bucket or small basket
Candle
Small soaps
White net
Ribbon about 1cm ($^3/_8$ in) wide
Lace about 5cm (2in) wide
Dried flowers

For gift bucket lined with fabric
Wooden bucket or small basket
Lace fabric
Lilac net
Tissue paper (optional)
Thin ribbon
Dried flowers

GIFT BUCKET WITH SOAPS AND CANDLE

1 Stand the candle in the centre of the container. To secure it in position, scrunch up lashings of net and push the net into the basket around the candle. For a bucket 15cm (6in) diameter, you will need about 1m (1yd), of net, though odd remnants work equally well. If necessary, glue the base of the candle in place.

2 Position the soaps on top of the net around the candle. Tease a little of the net up in between each soap so that it is visible.

3 Cut the dried flower stems into 5cm (2in) lengths and arrange in a circle around the candle, pushing the stems down into the net.

4 Cut a length of lace and ribbon to fit around the top of the container so it overlaps. Secure with double-sided tape at the back. Here, red ribbon has been woven through the eyelets of traditional lace.

GIFT BUCKET LINED WITH FABRIC

1 Cut one circle each of lace and net, two to three times bigger in diameter than your container. Line the bucket with fabric, placing the lace in first. Allow the excess to flop over the side.

2 Place small gifts in the middle of the bucket and if necessary protect or secure gifts with crunched-up tissue paper for padding. Gather up the fabric over the gifts, and secure with an elastic band (rubber band).

3 Cover the band with a thin ribbon tied into a bow. Finish with dried flowers and a bunch of lavender, slipping the stems behind the ribbon to secure into position. Trim the stems if necessary. Cut a length of ribbon to fit around the top of the bucket so that it overlaps. Secure with double-sided tape at the back.

VARIATIONS

• Rather than lace or ribbon, decorate the rim of a bucket with a length of ivy. Choose a piece (which is not too thick, or it won't be pliable) about eight centimetres (a few inches) longer than the circumference of the bucket. Twist the two ends where they overlap. If this does not hold the ivy in position, secure with small pieces of double-sided tape.

• Another very effective decorating technique using leaves is to apply laurel leaves around the rim of the bucket (see page 38) and finish with a raffia bow. Experiment with other evergreen leaves too.

• As a change from natural wood, opt for dramatic colours and paint the buckets with thick emulsion (latex) paint. Apply the paint in two coats, allowing it to dry between coats. If desired, add ribbons, buttons or other trimmings.

• Instead of net use layers of tissue paper or crepe paper, or for something truly opulent, use remnants of fabric in velvet, silk, gauze, lace or brocade and finish with silken tassels.

BASKETS OF FOOD

FOR FOOD LOVERS there's no more welcome present than a basket of mouthwatering goodies. Instead of spending a fortune on ready-made hampers, try making them yourself.

Although traditional hampers, filled with an assortment of seasonal foods, are delightful, themed gift baskets can be even more successful. Decide on one particular food, preferably one you are sure the recipient will enjoy, and then buy it in as many different forms and colours as possible. The ingredients don't need to be exotic or expensive, just the best and freshest.

The collection of food is then arranged in little bags, all presented in a basket. The number and size of bags you fill obviously depends on the size of the basket and the type of food.

It's important not to be mean when filling the bags – they should be almost overflowing. Three or four generously filled bags grouped together in a gift basket look better than a dozen or so bags only half-filled.

The pasta basket is great fun to assemble and is always popular. Everyone is always amazed at how many different types of pasta there are. It looks stunning and it's dead easy to make.

MATERIALS

Assortment of differently shaped and coloured dried pasta
Greaseproof paper or baking parchment
Scissors
Double-sided tape
Basket

1 To make each bag, cut a piece of greaseproof paper or baking parchment 25cm (10in) deep by 30cm (12in) wide.

2 Fold the paper so that the two side edges meet and just overlap. Secure at the back from top to bottom with double-sided tape.

3 Carefully fold all around the top edge twice, turning the folds outwards. This not only looks smart, but also prevents the bag from ripping.

4 Fold up the bottom edge of the paper twice, thus making a bag, and secure the edge with double-sided tape. Make enough of these bags to fill your basket.

5 Generously fill each bag with pasta, using as many different shapes and colours of pasta as you can find. Arrange the bags in the basket. If you wish, decorate the basket with a bow.

VARIATIONS

• In the summer, when the market stalls are laden with soft fruits, make a 'red berry' basket. Gather together strawberries, raspberries, cherries and other types of berries. Make some paper bags as explained in steps 1-4. Or if you have remnants of red and white gingham, make some simple fabric bags (see pages 60-1), lining them with greaseproof (waxed) paper, tissue paper or plain kitchen paper (paper towels). Fill the bags generously with the fruit. You could tie a piece of red or white ribbon around the neck of each bag.

• For someone with a sweet tooth, you could fill a basket with bags overflowing with colourful sugar candies. Make the bags out of an assortment of brightly coloured crepe paper – once they are filled, the result will be a wonderful kaleidoscope of colour. (Make these bags smaller than those for pasta, otherwise you will need a huge amount of sweets.)

• Instead of food, fill bags with bulbs – crocuses, snowdrops, hyacinths, tulips and daffodils. The bags could be arranged in a large, deep terracotta saucer, rather than a basket. Into each bag, slip planting instructions as well as the plant names. You might like to cut out relevant illustrations from a bulb catalogue. It makes a great present for a keen gardener.

GIFT BASKETS ON A THEME

INSTEAD OF BUYING a ready-made hamper or gift basket, you can have fun filling your own, making each one unique, or personalized for the recipient.

Baskets make wonderful containers for gifts, particularly for awkwardly shaped small objects or for a themed collection of little presents. Ribbons, tassels, an assortment of fabric and paper, dried flowers and fruit, foliage – all can be used to embellish a basket in next to no time and at very little expense.

As well as traditional woven baskets, which come in a multitude of shapes, sizes, and colours, containers such as garden trugs, wooden boxes, flowerpots or bamboo steamers can all be adapted.

One way to make your gift baskets unique is to create each one around a theme – for example, a gardener's planting basket, a bath basket, or a housewarming basket. A good starting point is to think of the recipient's favourite pleasures: a theme will quickly suggest itself.

Where possible, choose a container that will fit the theme of the gift; for example, embellished wooden sieves, jelly moulds and baking tins all make wonderful containers for a cooking or kitchen theme. Florists, fruit and vegetable markets and food shops (particularly Chinese and Indian supermarkets) are excellent sources of interesting containers. When you are decorating your basket or container, keep it simple and coordinate the colours, to guarantee that your gift is immediately eye-catching.

The packing of the container is also important. In order to make it pretty as well as practical, use lots of coloured tissue paper and cellophane in addition to lashings of net. A nice touch is to scatter potpourri among the packing. Or instead of packing materials you may prefer just to line the container with an attractive cloth or a piece of delicate lace.

COVERED BOXES

FABRIC CAN TRANSFORM a plain box, making it worthy of a really special gift. Yet all you need are a few pieces of fabric and a pot of glue. If you want to make your own cardboard box, see pages 58-9.

MATERIALS

Box
Fabric
Ruler
Set square
Scissors
Fabric glue

Avoid using fabrics that are heavy or have bumpy textures or that fray too easily – firmly woven cottons are ideal. For best results (and particularly if you are using a fabric patterned with a grid), cut out the pieces following the straight grain of the fabric. Use a ruler and set square to ensure your lines are straight and corners square.

1 Cut two pieces of fabric large enough to cover the ends of the box, adding an extra 1.5cm (5/8in) to each edge. Spread a thin layer of glue over the back of the fabric pieces and stick them onto the ends of the box. When gluing the fabric, make sure you smooth out any bubbles. Make vertical cuts into the excess fabric at the top and bottom edges. Fold over the fabric onto the inside, sides and base of the box, and stick it down *(above right)*.

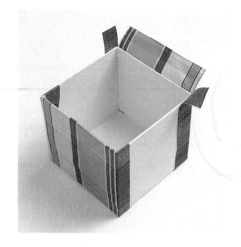

2 Cut two pieces of fabric to fit the sides of the box, adding an extra 1.5cm (5/8in) to the top and base edges only. Carefully glue the fabric pieces in place, folding the excess fabric onto the inside and the base of the box and sticking it down *(below)*. If you wish, cut a piece of fabric to fit the base of the box. Glue neatly in position.

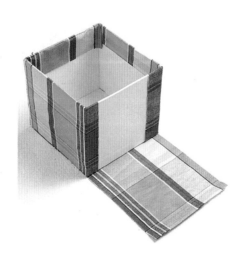

3 Cut one piece of fabric to fit over the top and sides of the lid, adding an extra 1.5cm (5/8in) to each edge. Spread glue over the top of the lid and position it centrally on the wrong side of the fabric. Make cuts into the extra fabric at the corners of two opposite sides. Glue the remaining fabric to the sides of the lid, folding the excess over to the inside of the rim and gluing it in place *(below)*.

VARIATIONS

• If you'd like a patchwork effect – or if you simply don't have enough of one particular material – try using two or more different fabrics. For best results the fabrics should be of a similar thickness.

• Instead of fabric you could cover boxes with good-quality wrapping paper, hand-made paper or wallpaper.

TEMPLATES

10cm (4in)

15cm (6in)

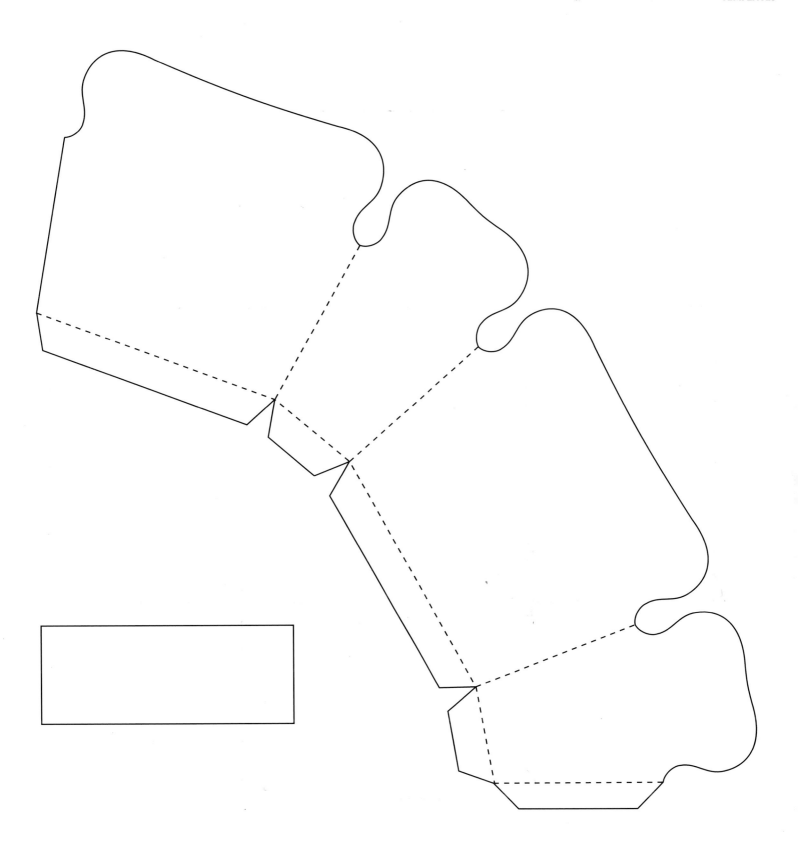

ACKNOWLEDGEMENTS

This book would not have been possible without the help and commitment of the following people. A very big thank you to Annabelle Lewis for her wonderful enthusiasm and help. A visit to her London shop, V V Rouleaux, stuffed full of every imaginable type of ribbon, is a must. I'd also like to thank Penny Duke of Paperchase, who guided me through a vast array of different papers, and David Scotcher, who generously gave me a supply of fabric remnants from his upholstery business.

I am indebted to Fiona Lindsay, my agent, for her constant guidance and encouragement, and to Suzannah Gough, who was involved in the birth of the idea.

In particular I wish to thank Nadia Mackenzie, who took all the glorious photographs and with whom I had such fun, Ian Pape of Thumb Design, who designed such a wonderful-looking book, and Alison Wormleighton, who so calmly and efficiently edited the text under near impossible deadlines. I am also grateful to Gabrielle Townsend at Weidenfeld & Nicolson who watched over the whole process and was always supportive.

And lastly, a very special thank you to Charles, who, as always, is a constant support and inspiration to me.

The ribbons used throughout this book were supplied by V V Rouleaux,
10 Symons Street, London SW3 2TJ. Tel: 0171-730 4413

Most of the materials used in this book were supplied by
Paperchase, 213 Tottenham Court Road,
London W1P 9AF. Tel: 0171-580 8496. (Branches or mail order).

INDEX